# WORLD WAR II
## SECRET O
# HANDBOOK

# WORLD WAR II
# SECRET OPERATIONS
# HANDBOOK

**S.O.E, O.S.S & MAQUIS GUIDE TO SABOTAGING THE NAZI WAR MACHINE**

## STEPHEN HART & CHRIS MANN

LYONS PRESS
Guilford, Connecticut

*An imprint of Globe Pequot Press*

To buy books in quantity for corporate use
or incentives, call **(800) 962–0973**
or e-mail **premiums@GlobePequot.com.**

Lyons Press is an imprint of Globe Pequot Press.

Library of Congress Cataloging-in-Publication Data is available on file.

ISBN: 978-0-7627-7986-4

Project Editor: Michael Spilling
Designer: Brian Rust
Illustrations: Tony Randell


Printed in Singapore

10 9 8 7 6 5 4 3 2 1

**DISCLAIMER**
**This book is for information purposes only. Readers should be aware of the legal position in**
**their country of residence before practicing any of the techniques described in this book.**
**Neither the author or the publisher can accept responsibility for any loss, injury, or damage**
**caused as a result of the use of the combat techniques described in this book, nor for any**
**prosecutions or proceedings brought or instigated against any person or body that may result**
**from using these techniques.**

# CONTENTS

# INTRODUCTION

**A**s World War II raged across the land-based fronts in Europe (and Southeast Asia), in the skies above and across the seas of these regions, another bitter struggle played out across some other, less obvious, front. This was the clandestine conflict waged by secret operatives – secret agents, spies or 'fourth columnists' – undertaking secret operations behind enemy lines to 'set Europe ablaze'. During this bitter cloak-and-dagger struggle, courageous secret operatives, having undergone specialized training and wielding ingenious equipment, pitted their wits against those of the enemy. These agents searched out the enemy's weaknesses and engaged them, thereby making a significant contribution to the war's eventual outcome.

All combatants of World War II developed dedicated organizations to control the behind-the-lines operations waged by special operatives. The United Kingdom's principal such organization was the Special Operations Executive (SOE), although the Special Intelligence Services (SIS) also undertook secret agent missions. The United States' equivalent was the Office for Strategic Services (OSS), while the Gaullist French regime-in-exile developed the Central Bureau of Intelligence and Operations (BCRA). Finally, in Nazi-occupied Europe local Resistance networks emerged that also fought (often with the help of SOE, OSS and BCRA) a clandestine partisan struggle against their Axis occupiers. These movements included the Maquis in occupied France, PAN in The Netherlands, Milorg in Norway, ELAS, EDES and EKKA in Greece, and the Partisans in the Soviet Union. Finally, in Hitler's Reich the armed forces counter-intelligence agency (*Abwehr*), the Nazi Party's SS Security Service (*Sicherheitsdienst* – the SD) and the Secret State Police (*Gestapo*) spearheaded Germany's own secret operative war.

## Secret Operations Techniques

But how did these secret operatives wage this cloak-and-dagger struggle against the enemy behind its own lines? This is what this work sets out to explain. It investigates the strategies, organization, tactics, techniques, skills, training, weapons, equipment, communication devices, operations, missions and intelligence that underpinned this desperate life-and-death struggle.

The *World War II Secret Operations Handbook* takes you deep into the murky covert world

# Main Gestapo HQs in Occupied Europe

The security services of the German occupation forces inevitably tended to establish themselves in the existing centres of power. The Gestapo (Secret State Police) along with the Nazi Party's Security Service (*Sicherheitsdienst*) under the umbrella of the Reich Security Main Office (*Reichssicherheitshauptamt* – RHSA) was no exception, establishing a major office in most capital and some major regional cities.

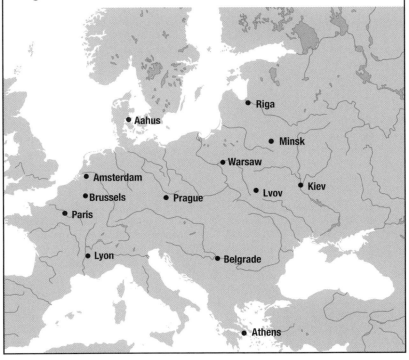

of the secret operative. Often, this is a fantastical world, filled with awe-inspiring human courage, bizarre technological gadgets, amazing specialized skills, cutting-edge training, and the human arts of ingenuity, guile and deception.

Ever wondered how a functional pistol could be designed to fit into an agent's belt buckle? Have you mused on how an agent might escape from his prison cell using only discarded cans of sardines? Want to know what an agent might need to add to cement mix to render enemy concrete fortifications fragile? Ever pondered on how an operative can overpower a vigilant armed guard, and kill him using his/her bare hands?

This work tells you how to do all this, and much more besides. It unravels the key techniques involved in the secret operative's deadly trade and describes some of the most important missions undertaken using these skills.

## Chapter Breakdown

Each of the seven chapters in the *World War II Secret Operations Handbook* examines one part of the typical covert mission cycle. Chapter 1 ('Insertion') examines the techniques and tactics employed to insert secret operatives into enemy-held territory. This explains how an agent was successfully inserted at night by light aircraft onto a small

improvised grass landing strip, or by submarine and canoe onto a deserted shoreline.

Chapter 2 ('Behind Enemy Lines') investigates the methods by which secret operatives lived off the land and survived behind enemy lines. It recounts how agents obtained food and water, made shelters, kindled fire for warmth and cooking, navigated by the stars, and a whole host of associated techniques that they used to survive.

Chapter 3 ('Working Undercover') describes how agents were able to operate behind enemy lines. This recounts how operatives made contact with local Resistance groups, rigged-up makeshift radios, worked out security procedures to foil enemy countermeasures, and other practical operational details.

Next, Chapter 4 ('Intelligence Gathering') analyzes the ways in which operatives gathered information about the enemy. It discusses the skills and techniques involved in effective visual surveillance of a target, and the tactics of telephone tapping.

Chapter 5 ('Sabotage') and Chapter 6 ('Combat') explain how operatives took the fight to the enemy. The first of these chapters examines the methods employed to sabotage enemy installations. It investigates the methods operatives employed to disrupt an enemy railway system, disable

# In the Shadows

**When crossing a road or any open space, agents and Resistance fighters took advantage of shadows thrown by trees, buildings and other features.**

an enemy tank factory, and render enemy concrete fortifications brittle.

The next chapter explains how secret operatives carried out assassination strikes against key enemy leaders, mounted ambushes and raids on enemy forces, and assisted the guerrilla warfare waged by local Resistance groups.

Finally, Chapter 7 ('Extraction') explores how operatives escaped from the scene after executing their mission, how they were then extracted from enemy territory back to home soil and, if they were unfortunate enough to be captured, the methods they employed to escape from captivity.

# Norwegian Resistance Weapons

**The Norwegian resistance were well supplied by the Allies. Kit for fighting units included the US-made M1 carbine, which was an ideal weapon for firefights at a distance of a few hundred metres.**

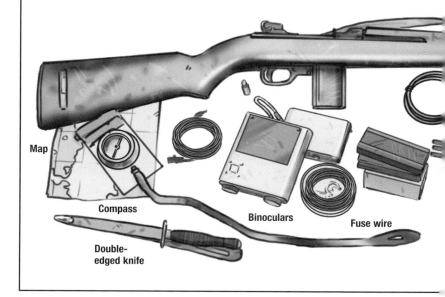

Map

Compass

Binoculars

Fuse wire

Double-edged knife

## Tips and Profiles

In addition to the main text, each chapter has a number of box features that describe in more detail certain aspects of these secret operations. There are four types of box feature in this work:

*Mission Profile* presents an in-depth account of a particular operative mission, such as the SOE plot to assassinate Hitler; *Tactics Tip* explains how a particular operative method was employed, such as assassination using a mine;

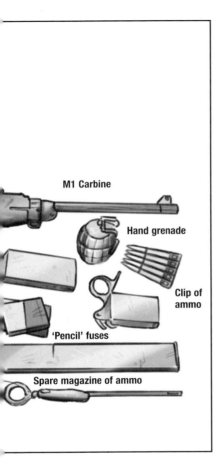

**M1 Carbine**

**Hand grenade**

**Clip of ammo**

**'Pencil' fuses**

**Spare magazine of ammo**

war's most (in)famous operatives, such as 'The She-Cat'.

The work is also illustrated with numerous captioned black-and-white diagrams or line drawings that shed extra light on the secret operative weapons, equipment, tactics, techniques, skills, training and missions discussed in the main text and sidebars.

The *World War II Secret Operations Handbook*, therefore, covers a wide spectrum of the techniques and skills employed during the operative's secret war that raged behind enemy lines. These ranged from the mundane, such as how an operative camouflaged his/her face, to the fantastical – how explosive tyre-bursters were made to resemble cow dung of the correct colour and texture for the local area in which they would be used. They scaled the heights of human endeavour: battered operatives held in Nazi concentration camps like Dachau somehow managing to escape; and plumbed the depths of duplicity: just who, precisely, was the *treble* agent 'The She-Cat' actually working for?

All this and more await those who turn these fascintaing pages; unlike many operatives in the field, however, after reading their secret instructions, you the reader will not be required to destroy these pages after finishing them!

*Equipment Profile* investigates the technical detail of a particular piece of operative equipment and how it was employed, such as the Westland Lysander light aircraft; finally, *Operative Profile* provides a brief résumé of some of the

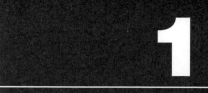

**B** y the late summer of 1940 the newly formed Special Operations Executive (SOE) faced considerable difficulty in 'setting Europe ablaze' given that British forces had been ejected from the Continent following the evacuation from Dunkirk and subsequent fall of France. Thus virtually all efforts to undertake covert action in Nazi-occupied Europe required the insertion of agents from the United Kingdom and this meant crossing the Channel or, in the case of Norway, the North Sea. Thus SOE developed a whole series of techniques for transporting its members and equipment for the European resistance members it was supporting by sea and by air. The organization became skilled in the use of boats, submarines and aircraft, either landing or making drops by parachute.

The situation changed once Allied forces returned to mainland Europe via Italy in the autumn of 1943 and then into Normandy in June 1944. Although aircraft remained the mainstay for inserting agents and resupply, other, more traditional,

. . . . . . . . . . . . . . . . . . . . . . . . . . . . . . . .

**Insertion into occupied territory could be carried out via land, sea or air. This would often involve the use of special technology, such as an S-phone or Welfreighter boat.**

**Inserting agents and resistance fighters into enemy territory can be one of the most difficult and potentially hazardous parts of any clandestine operation.**

means of moving through enemy lines and into their rear areas could be used. For the Soviets this was always the situation. In the campaign following the German invasion of June 1941, as the need to move through frontline areas was a constant requirement for Soviet Partisans, great consideration was given to the best means by which to cross through the front line.

## By Air

For SOE, the key delivery system of both agents and supplies was the aircraft. There were two methods: the agent could be dropped off by a plane which had landed or make a parachute jump. Both had advantages and disadvantages. Parachuting meant less risk to the aircraft but did mean that agents and supplies might be scattered, damaged or both. Landing put the aircraft and pilot in greater danger, but allowed for greater precision and made injury to passengers and damage to equipment less likely. It also meant that verbal messages could be passed and agents extracted on the same trip.

At the end of Group A training prospective agents took the parachute course at Special Training School (STS) 51 at Manchester's Ringway airfield. Agents' first sessions were spent being dropped from special harnesses on to crash mats to simulate landings. This then

progressed to jumping from a 23m (75ft) tower and then to a static balloon 213m (700ft) up. Finally, there came three daylight drops from an aircraft and two at night. The students needed to master basic parachute landing technique and learn the necessity of keeping both legs together to lessen the chance of breaking something. This had to become instinctive as there would be no time to think when the time came for real.

### Aircraft Employed

The aircraft that operated in support of SOE were usually obsolete or obsolescent bombers. The RAF's Bomber Command was loath to equip the squadrons that supported SOE with modern aircraft. Air Chief Marshal Sir Charles Portal, Chief of the Air Staff, told SOE that 'your work is a gamble which may give us valuable dividend or may produce nothing. It is anybody's guess. My bombing offensive is not a gamble, its dividend is certain; it is a gilt edged investment. I cannot divert aircraft from a certainty to a gamble which may be a gold-mine or may be completely worthless.' As a result, the number of available aircraft was small, certainly in comparison to the vast bomber fleets sent against Germany and other targets in occupied Europe.

Only five British-based aircraft were to work with the Resistance until August 1941. By the end of

# Allied Aircraft Types

**RAF support for SOE was largely in the form of its ageing heavy bombers. Initially, the Whitley and later aircraft such as the Wellington and Halifax dropped agents and supplies across Europe.**

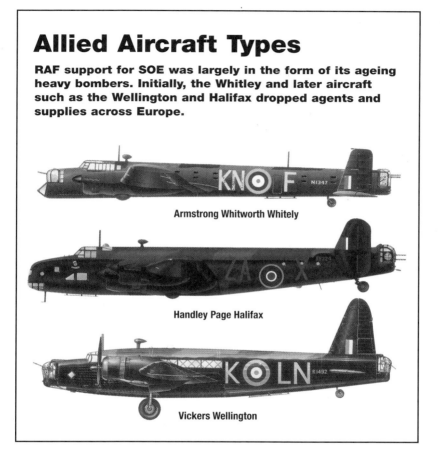

Armstrong Whitworth Whitely

Handley Page Halifax

Vickers Wellington

the following year it was still under 30 and the number of aircraft available to SOE on a full-time basis never passed 60. Two squadrons, No. 138 and No. 161, undertook the missions from a carefully disguised aerodrome at Templeford near Cambridge.

Occasionally, the base at Tangemere in Kent was made available and extra support could occasionally be loaned from Transport or Bomber Command. The USAAF added two more squadrons flying Liberators and Dakotas in January 1944.

# Equipment Profile:
# The Westland Lysander
# Mark III

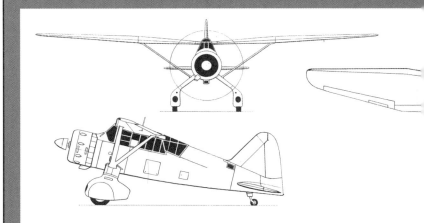

The Westland Lysander was designed as an army cooperation and light support aircraft. It entered service in 1938 and saw action in France in 1940, which exposed its limitations as a frontline combat aircraft. However, the 'Lizzie', as it was known, really came into its own as a support aircraft for SOE and Britain's intelligence services. The aircraft's sturdiness, manoeuvrability and extraordinary ability to take off

So, when planning air drops, the relative working radii of the aircraft had to be taken into account. The Armstrong Whitworth Whitley could operate out to about 1368km (850 miles), the Vickers Wellington had a slightly shorter range, and the Handley-Page Halifax, a few of

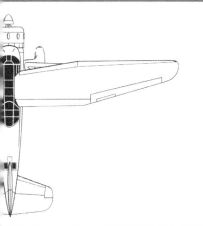

**Crew:** 1
**Passengers:** 1–2 (3 at most).
**Powerplant:** One 649kW (870hp) Bristol Mercury XX 9-cylinder air-cooled radial engine.
**Performance:** Maximum speed 341km/h (212mph) at 1525m (5000ft); service ceiling 6555m (21,500ft).
**Fuel Capacity:** 482 litres (106 Imperial gallons) in a fuselage tank. The Lysander Mk IIISCW could carry an external long-range tank of 150 Imperial gallons (682 litres) could also be carried to extend the range.
**Range:** 966km (600 miles) on internal fuel; 1448km (900 miles) with external tank.
**Weight:** Empty 1980kg (4365lbs) with a maximum take-off weight of 2865kg (6318lbs).
**Wing Span:** 15.24m (50ft).
**Length:** 9.3m (30ft 6in).

and land within a small area made it ideal for clandestine work. As SOE's official historian, M.R.D. Foot wrote, 'as Voltaire said of God, that had it not existed it would have had to have been invented'.

which were added to Nos 138 and 161 Squadrons' roster from August 1941, had a similar range too. The Liberators used by the USAAF could reach a couple of hundred miles further. For landing agents, the preferred aircraft was the Westland Lysander, an aircraft designed for reconnaissance and artillery spotting. It was perfect for delivering agents, being sturdy, manoeuvrable and having superb short take-off and landing capabilities, although being a much smaller single-engined aircraft, its operational radius was a much shorter 724km (450 miles).

SOE also used the Lockheed Hudson, a much larger twin-engined light bomber in this role. It could carry a Rebecca airborne receiver for the Eureka homing beacon and comfortably carry 12 men or a ton of stores. However, it required a kilometre or so of flat meadow in which to land and take off. So the range of these aircraft meant that large areas of Eastern Europe, such as eastern Poland, Finland and the USSR, which was particularly wary of aircraft operating for foreign secret services anyway, were outside SOE's supporting aircrafts' range.

The following section is adapted from 'The SOE Syllabus: Selection of Dropping Points and Landing Sites, July 1943', in *How to be a Spy: The SOE Training Manual*.

# Selection of the Drop Zone

The reception committee is responsible for selecting the drop zone. This must meet certain basic principles. Dropping operations take place on moonlit nights by aircraft flying between 152 and 182m (500 and 600ft) at 160–193km/h (100–120

mph). Therefore, an open area of ground not less than 548m (600 yards) square is required. This should be increased to at least 731m (800 yards), if several containers or men are being dropped. This area will be sufficient, whatever the wind direction. Drops should not take place if the wind speed is above 32km/h (20mph). Agricultural ground and swamps should be avoided. Ploughed fields are a physical hazard to landing parachutists and damage to the crops might leave evidence of the landing. The area should be free of telegraph or high-tension wires. While cover in the immediate vicinity is an advantage, high trees are also a hazard to be avoided.

The selection of the site must always take into consideration three major concerns:
1) The safety of the dropping aircraft.
2) The site's easy recognizability at night.
3) The planning and make-up of the reception committee.

## Aircraft Safety

To ensure the safety of the aircraft three main points should be observed:
1) The area should be away from heavily defended areas, to avoid flak concentrations. Enemy aerodromes are particularly dangerous and should be avoided at all costs.
2) The selected area should be as level as possible. Mountainous and high country should be avoided if

possible, but a high plateau might be usable if it meets the correct dimensions. Valleys should also be avoided unless particularly wide.
3) The dropping aircraft must be clear of enemy territory by daybreak and, therefore, travelling times and distances (usually from the UK) must be taken into consideration.

## Recognizability of Site

To ensure the site's recognizability at night the following issues should be taken into consideration. A pilot flying at 1828m (6000 feet) on a moonlit night should easily be able to spot the following points to aid navigation:
1) The coastline, if possible with breaking surf; and river mouths over 47m (50 yards) wide.
2) Rivers and canals. Both provide moon reflection, which is helpful. Wooded banks may reduce this. A river needs to be at least 27m (30 yards) wide. This is less important with regard to canals as their unnatural straightness will aid identification. There is a danger of misidentification if the area is crisscrossed with numerous rivers.
3) Large lakes, at least half a mile wide. Care should be taken if there is more than one in the area.
4) Forests and wood blocks. Need to be at least 0.8km (0.5 miles) wide and of a regular shape. Consult a recent map in case of recent felling, which might have altered the profile.
5) Straight roads, at least 1.6km

(1 mile) in length, are good navigation guides, particularly when wet. Narrow or winding lanes are of no use.
6) Railway lines. Only useful in winter when snow is on the ground as a main line cuts a distinctive black ribbon across the landscape.
7) Towns and built-up areas. In conditions of black-out, towns are unlikely to be of much use unless over the size of 20,000 inhabitants. One needs to consider the possibility of anti-aircraft defences.

It is clear, therefore, that areas of water provide the best points for quick recognition. The ideal is to have a combination of distinctive features, the last of which should not be more than 4.8km (3 miles) away from the dropping point. The drop zone itself should be marked by a system of ground lighting (see below).

It is essential that the air point of view take precedence, as it is the pilot who must make the drop. Gaining a literal 'bird's-eye view' is virtually impossible, so the drop zone has to be located on a map and then a reconnaissance undertaken to confirm the site's suitability. It is worth choosing a large number of sites, maybe as many as 20 or 30. While examining a large-scale map, a number of factors should be taken into consideration:
1) Contours and thereby the gradients.
2) The nature of the ground, i.e. marsh, heathland, woodland etc.
3) The extent/size of possible landing/drop zones.

# Recognizability of Site

The pilot needed to be guided to the drop zone via recognizable landmarks. Water features such as the coastline, lakes and canals were best but wooded areas, towns and major road and rail links could also be used.

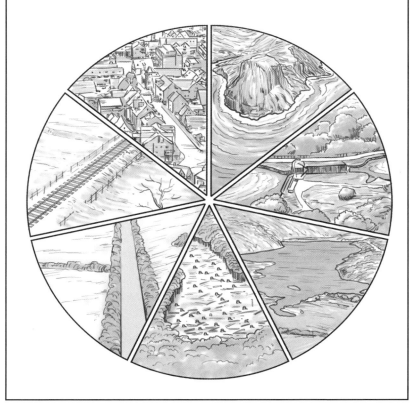

# Examining a Map

**The initial selection of a site would be done on a map, checking the gradient, nature of the ground and the presence of habitation or hazards such as water or high-tension wires.**

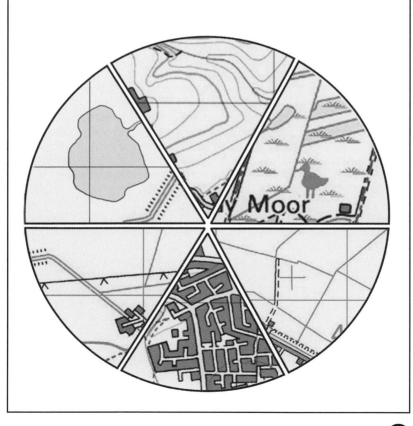

# Container Types

The drop will be made during bright moonlight in the period of five to six days either side of a full moon. Drop zones within 32km (20 miles) of the coast may be used for slightly longer periods. The reception committee needs to be available for five consecutive nights given the vagaries of this type of operation. Enough men were required to provide security and move the dropped containers. Once a request is put into headquarters, the process of organizing a drop will take at least 14 days.

The C Type containers used are 172cm by 238cm (5' 8" by 15") – about the size of a man – and weigh 43kg (96lbs) unloaded. H Type containers are slightly smaller, at 167cm by 38cm (5' 6" by 15") diameter and 4.5kg (10lbs) lighter. They contain four cells loaded with equipment and esily requires six men to handle it. A spade is usually attached for the purpose of burying the container after it is emptied. Throwing it into a suitably deep lake or river also works well. Apparently, the containers make good targets for shooting practice, but this is not encouraged by London.

Type H containers carry five different standard loads:

H1: Explosives and accessories.
H2: Sten sub-machine guns.
H3: Weapons.
H4: Incendiary material.
H5: Sabotage material.

Thus a very short message is required to place an order, for example 'send 2 H1 and 4 H2'.

[Taken from 'The SOE Syllabus: Selection of Dropping Points and Landing Sites, July 1943', in *How to be a Spy: The SOE Training Manual,* Toronto: Dundurn, 2001.]

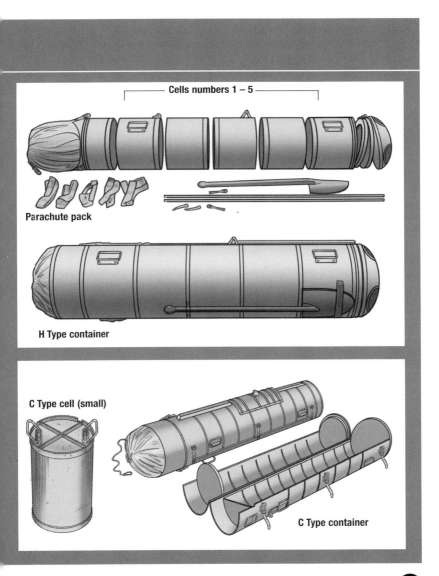

Cells numbers 1 – 5

Parachute pack

H Type container

C Type cell (small)

C Type container

4) Habitation in the vicinity.
5) High-tension wire and other hazards.
6) Expanses of water, rivers, lakes and canals.

Suitable sites should be reported back to headquarters using conventional map references.

## Considerations for Pilots

So, presuming a suitable location was found, a request for an air drop made, the request accepted and appropriate reception party organized, all that was needed was for the aircraft to find the drop zone safely. Wing Commander H.S. Verity provided notes and advice for Lysander and Hudson pilots on operations such as these. They are also useful for anyone undertaking a navigation exercise. He reckoned that: 'By far the greatest of work you do to carry out a successful pick-up happens before you leave the ground' and 'Never get over-confident about your navigation … Each operation should be prepared with as much care as your first, however experienced you may be.'

His thoughts on choosing the route in and navigation very much mirrored the SOE's advice for selecting drop zones. Once the target was established, it was necessary to pick a 'really good landmark nearby'. Then a route needed to be worked out, 'hopping from landmark to landmark' while avoiding possible flak concentrations. 'Try to arrange a really good landmark at each turning point, for example a coast or a big river.' He recommended spending 'two hours in an armchair reading your maps before you go'. Know the terrain either side of the route, try to memorize the shape and patterns of woods and towns and 'the way in which other landmarks converge on them'.

### Preparation

With regard to loading the aircraft – Verity was referring specifically to the Westland Lysander, the mainstay of SOE agent pick-up/drop-off operations (see *Equipment Profile: The Westland Lysander Mark III*, p16) – it was possible to get four passengers in, although three was the normal recommended maximum and 'as you can well imagine, that means a squash'. The heaviest luggage should be stowed under the seat nearest the centre of gravity. Important items 'such as sacks of money, should go on the shelf, so they are not left in the aeroplane by mistake'. It is not difficult to imagine how easy it was to forget or mislay something while hastily exiting an aircraft in the middle of a darkened field in the middle of occupied territory. The amount of fuel carried affected the aircraft's handling characteristics, particularly when taking off and landing. Yet it was advisable to have 'a very large margin of safety' of enough fuel for about two hours extra flying time, as 'you may well be kept waiting an hour or more in the target area by a reception committee that is late turning up' or you might get lost.

Verity's remarks on personal emergency kit are apposite:

*If you get stuck in the mud, it is useful to have in the aeroplane some civilian clothes … You should also carry a standard escape, some purses of French money, a gun or two, and a thermos flask of hot coffee or*

# Dead Reckoning (DR)

**Dead reckoning was an important part of any World War II pilot's navigational process. Essentially, the pilot or navigator would work out where his speed and compass bearing should take him over his flight plan and then hope to marry up that information with the map and the ground below him. Wind speed and direction would be taken into consideration. It was an absolutely vital navigational tool and usually checked at least once every 483km (300 miles).**

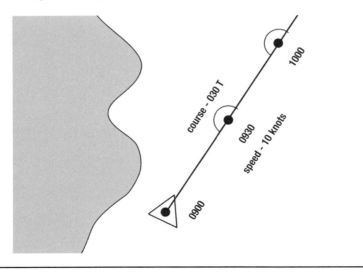

*what you will. A small flask of brandy or whisky is useful if you have to swim for it, but NOT in the air. Empty your pockets of anything of interest to the Hun, but carry with you some small photographs of yourself in civilian clothes. These may be attached to false identity papers. In theory it is wise to wear clothes with no tailor's, laundry or personal marks. Change your linen before flying, as dirty shirts have a bad effect on wounds. The Lysander is a warm aircraft, and I always wore a pair of shoes rather than flying boots. If you have to walk across the Pyrenees you might as well do it in comfort.*

Thus prepared, he recommended that after a nap in afternoon, as 'it is most important to start an op fresh', finally you should ensure that 'you get driven to your aeroplane in a smart American car … cluttered up from head to toe with equipment and arms and kit of every description,

# Landing and Take-off Pattern

**The pilot flying into the wind would aim to touch the ground at about point A. He would break and then turn between lights B and C and then taxi back to point A and stop to the right of A. Then, a drop-off or pick-up would be undertaken before the pilot took off – facing into the wind.**

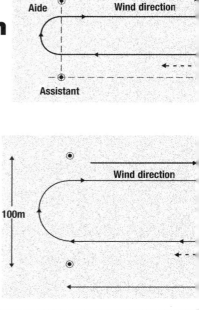

rather like the White Knight, prepared for every emergency'.

## The Flight Out

Before take-off it was essential to ensure 'the agent knows the form'. It was essential that he knew how much luggage he was carrying and where it was stowed, where the parachutes were, how the internal communication system worked and the drill for landing. If the Lysander was both dropping off and picking up agents, there was a set method for the turn around. One agent would stay in the aircraft to hand out his own luggage and then receive the kit of the homecoming agent, before getting out himself.

Once airborne, Verity preferred to cross the Channel high to avoid trigger-happy members of the Royal Navy and flak from enemy coastal convoys, and in any case, if flying low, it took a long time for a heavily laden Lysander to reach his preferred height for crossing the enemy coast as high as possible at about 2438m

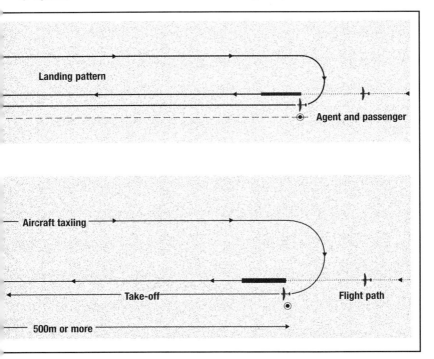

(8000ft). This gave a good general view and ruled out the danger of light flak. Once the point of crossing was identified, 'you may gaily climb above any low cloud there may be and strike into the interior on Dead Reckoning (DR)'.

Verity warned of the dangers of misidentifying a landmark, 'so never have faith in one pin point until you have checked with a second or even a third, nearby'. When it came to identifying landmarks, he broadly concurred with SOE's instructions. As he said, 'water always shows up better than anything else, even in very poor light'. Forests and woods were next best and often made 'very good landmarks', particularly if large. He was slightly more positive about railways than SOE. While admitting that 'a railway may not be very easily seen in itself, the lie of the track may be deduced from the contours of the land' or 'given away by the glowing firebox of an engine'. However, the real advantage of railways 'is that they are few and far between and therefore less likely to be confused with each other'.

Roads on the other hand 'can be very confusing, because there are often many more on the ground than are marked on you map'. The route nationale, 'lined with poplars and driving practically straight across country', could be useful and roads were a reasonable way to find a town or village. However, 'in general

terms it is wiser to use roads as a check on other landmarks'. Large towns should be avoid 'on principle' in case of flak. 'This is a pity, of course, because large towns are very good landmarks.'

## The Landing

On the approach to the target area, after running through the cockpit drill and putting the signalling lamp to Morse 'and generally waking yourself up', it was time to locate the landing field. 'Don't be lured away from your navigation by the siren call of stray lights', he warned. 'You should aim to find the field without depending on lights and be prepared to circle and look for it. If the approach is made straightaway the signal may be missed because it is given directly beneath the plane. Once the light is seen, identify the Morse letter being flashed is correct.' Once again, Verity warned:

> If the letter is not correct, or if there is any irregularity in the flare path or if the field is not the one you expected, you are in NO circumstances to land. There have been cases when the Germans have tried to make a Lysander land, but the pilot has got away with it by following this very strict rule. In one case where this rule was disobeyed, the pilot came home with thirty bullet holes in his aircraft and one in his neck, and

# Landing Using Landmarks

**More skilful pilots could land their aircraft in a hidden location, such as between rows of trees or bushes. But such manoeuvres were only possible if the landing took place during daylight, which brought many dangers, including detection by enemy ground forces and threats from enemy fighter aircraft.**

# Typical Ground Beacon Layout at the Drop Zone

**In an open field about 607–914m (2000–3000ft) long, three red lights would be set up 91m (300ft) apart, with a fourth white light set up perpendicular to the third light. This light would flash the morse recognition signal. The dropping plane would approach at 152m (500ft) on the drop axis against the wind as slowly as possible and would begin dropping the containers on the second light.**

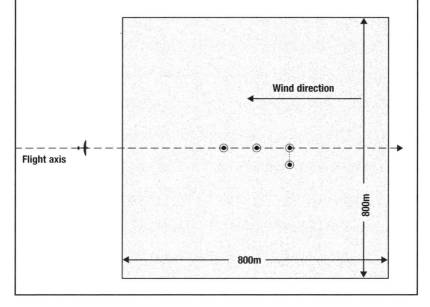

only escaped with his life because he landed far from the flare path and took off again at once. Experience has shown that a

German ambush on the field will not open fire until the aeroplane attempts to take-off having landed. Their object is to get you *alive to get the gen, so don't be tricked into a sense of security if you are not shot at from the field before landing. I repeat, the entire lighting procedure must be correct before you even think of landing.*

The actual landing was something that would have been practised time and time again in training. 'On your first operation', Verity reckoned, 'you will be struck by the similarity of the flare path to the training flare path and until you are very experienced you take your time and make a job of it'. The first thing to do was to take a compass bearing on the landing lights and circle and check all the lights were where they were expected to be.

'The approach in should be steep to avoid trees or obstacles', Verity added. 'You should not touch down before the first landing light or more than 50 yards [46m] beyond it. Use the landing light if necessary in the last few seconds but turn it off the moment the aircraft touches the ground. Taxi to the light where the agent will be standing and then turn the plane around so it points back the way for take-off.'

Verity counselled that: 'At this point you may be in something of a flap but don't forget any letters or messages you may have been given for the agent.' Once given the okay, it was a case of – 'off you go'.

## The Flight Back

On the return journey, it was very important not to relax and forget the importance of navigation on the way back, as it was necessary to avoid flak concentrations. One could not 'just point your nose in the direction of home. … for the sake of your passengers, you should not get shot down on the way back. So navigate all the way there and back.' In double pick-ups, Verity advised caution in radio communications, as 'German wireless intelligence is probably listening with some interest to your remarks', so no reference other than code words should be made to the landing area.

In conclusion, Verity noted the 'good will which exists between pilots and agents' and that 'all pilots should realise what a tough job the agents take on and try to get to know them and give them confidence in pick-up operations'.

He recognized that this could be difficult 'if you don't speak French and the agent doesn't speak English, but don't be shy and do your best to get to know your trainees and passengers and let them get to know you'. He finally pointed out that such operations are 'perfectly normal forms of war transport' and should not be mythologized as if they were 'a sort of trick-cycling spectacle'. Professionalism and proper preparation should ensure success on virtually every occasion.

# Operative Profile: Wing Commander Hugh Verity (1918–2001)

Hugh Verity joined the RAF shortly after the outbreak of World War II. In the winter of 1942, after service with RAF reconnaissance and night fighter squadrons, he volunteered for No. 161 Squadron, which supported SOE operations, and was accepted. He went on to fly around 30 Lysander missions into France, once with Jean Moulin, leader of the Gaullist Resistance, as passenger. He was a skilled, resourceful and determined pilot. He was also popular with his charges and the reception committees on the ground due to his calm, friendly demeanour, helped not least by his ability to speak French. Verity was awarded the DFC and DSO for his exploits and the Legion d'Honneur in 1946. He later became an SOE air operations officer organizing drops and landings across Western Europe and Scandinavia, and in the autumn of 1944 moved to Southeast Asia to supervise clandestine air operations there. He continued to serve in the RAF after the war before retiring in 1965.

## Guiding the Aircraft into the Target Area

These operations needed a direct link between the men on the ground and the air crew. Once Verity or one of his colleagues had located the drop or landing zone, the whole process was much facilitated if ground-to-air communications were available. Landing lights could do the job. In remote areas of the Balkans bonfires could be used. These, however, left evidence. Cans or containers filled with sand and dosed in petrol or paraffin could be used; these were easily doused and carried away in case of emergency. In most of Europe more discreet methods were generally used. The light signals used had to be visible from the air but must not alert hostile forces in the vicinity on the ground. The usual method was to use domestic torches or bicycle lamps. SOE supplied modified Eveready two-cell torches, which were adequate if not really robust enough. Experiments showed on a clear night four days after a ful moon an aircraft flying at 305m (1000ft) could see a visual signal at a range of 8km (5 miles). Coloured filters – red, amber, green and blue – were issued with the torches; and of these, red and green were the easiest to spot. Lighting on the field was absolutely central to landing an aircraft or conducting a parachute drop, but the whole process was

# Using an S-Phone Type 13/MkIV (1943)

**The S-Phone was remarkably easy to use, functioning in essentially the same way as a telephone. That said, the set was directional and the operator had to be facing into the path of the oncoming aircraft.**

# Equipment Profile:
# S-Phone

### Specifications
**Transmission frequency**: 337 megacycles.
**Reception frequency**: 380 megacycles.
**Power output**: 0.1–0.2 watt.

**Dimensions**: 19 x 10 x 50cm (7.5 x 4 x 20in).
**Weight**: 1kg (2.25lbs).
**Total weight**: 7.7kg (17lbs) (including harness, batteries etc)

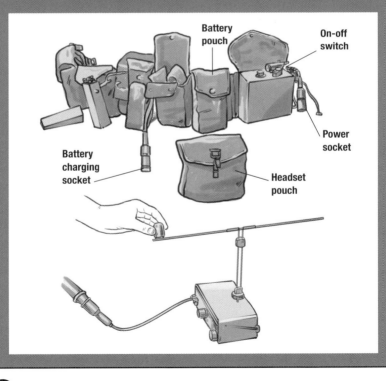

Battery pouch

On-off switch

Power socket

Battery charging socket

Headset pouch

much facilitated by the introduction of the S-Phone, a shortwave radio telephone that allowed the aircraft (or ship) to home in on the ground station (carried in the pack of the operator) and also pass verbal messages·between pilot and operator. It could be fairly easily carried by the man on the ground but could not really be explained away if caught in possession of the device by the enemy.

## Use of the S-Phone

The S-Phone could be used for three distinct purposes: radiotelephone, homing beacon and parachute drop spot indicator.

The SOE equipment manual noted that the use of high frequencies to provide low-power communication between ground and aircraft had real advantages with regard to security:

1) Radio energy at [the above] frequencies will not pass through major obstacles, but requires what is an almost 'optical' path for transmission and reception consequently an intercept station must be sited on an unobstructed path from the transmitter.

2) Transmission and reception uses two separate frequency channels, therefore interception would have to be accomplished with two separately tuned receivers in order to hear both sides of the conversation.

3) Intercept stations are very rarely provided with receiving equipment working at the extremely high frequencies used.

4) Range is dependent on the height of the aerials above 'ground'. 'Ground Range' is very limited and so reduces the possibility of interception.

Thus it was about as secure as such a system could be: a ground monitor station would have to be within a mile to pick up the signal. It was also pretty straightforward, as according to SOE 'any intelligent person is able to use the apparatus with the minimum of instruction'. The set itself was held under a belt by two webbed straps. A vertical dipole was unfolded and then plugged into its socket on the chest box. The operator adjusted the frequency knob on the base of the chest box with his right hand to get the best reception.

The webbing rig contained seven canvas pouches. Five of these held the 10 miniature batteries, the sixth the vibrator power pack and the seventh was for the headset, microphone and aerial when not in use. The microphone and headphone were attached to the transmitter receiver by a flexible cable and heavy-duty plug and socket. The headset and microphone, which 'restricts vocal radiation', meant that the system was virtually soundproof.

The S-Phone was a duplex transceiver, so there was no

# Communication Links

**The S-Phone offered remarkable flexibility with regard to communications: secure ship-to-ship, ground-to-sea, ground-to-air, air-to-ground and sea-to-air links. The direction indicators on the ground set allowed aircraft and ships to home in on the signal, allowing a degree of tactical flexibility.**

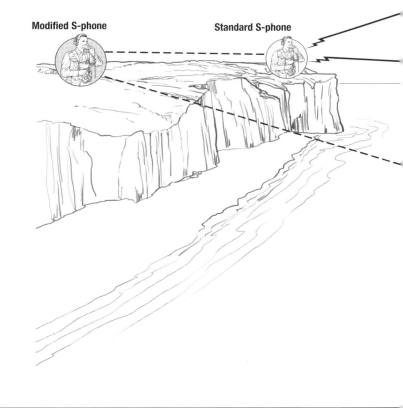

Modified S-phone

Standard S-phone

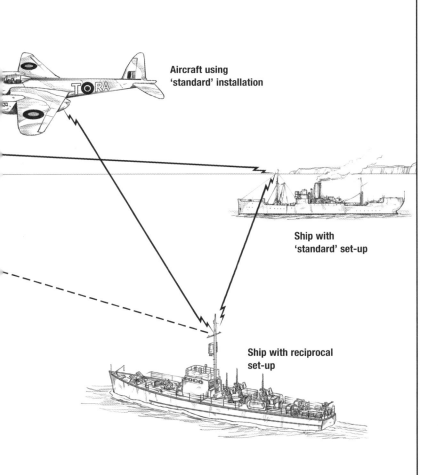

Aircraft using
'standard' installation

Ship with
'standard' set-up

Ship with reciprocal
set-up

# Ground-to-air Communication

**The S-Phone was markedly directional and its range increased with the altitude of the incoming aircraft. If the aircraft turned within the beam at high altitude, communications could be maintained, allowing voice recognition, such was the quality of transmission.**

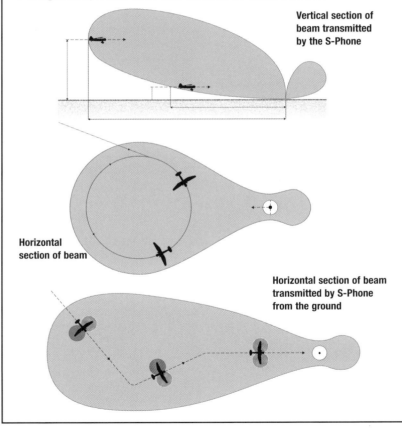

Vertical section of beam transmitted by the S-Phone

Horizontal section of beam

Horizontal section of beam transmitted by S-Phone from the ground

switching from send to receive; in fact, the conversation between aircraft and operator could be conducted just as it would be by ordinary telephone. The quality of the voice communication was such that the voice of the operator could be recognized.

The set was directional and the operator had to face the direction from which the aircraft approached, but this allowed the aircraft to fly straight towards the speaker, an immense help in locating drop zones in difficult terrain. When used as a homing beacon the maximum range was about 97km (60 miles) at 3045m (10,000ft). By the time the range had closed to 48–64km (30–40 miles), communication could be established.

## The Eureka/Rebecca Radar System

The Eureka/Rebecca radar guidance system appeared a little later in the war, being first deployed in early 1942. Eureka was the ground-based radar beacon set up in the drop or landing zone. Rebecca was the receiver carried by the aircraft, although its 7.6m (25ft) long aerial proved too large for the Lysander.

The Eureka set was pretty hefty too as it weighed about 49kg (110lbs) and the carrying box was 76 x 38 x 25cm (30 x 15 x 10in). So it was man-portable … just. It was, at least, easy to use. The Eureka beacon

had a 1.5m (5ft) retractable mast on a 2.1m (7ft) tripod, and was connected to a totally enclosed box. All that had to be done was for it to be turned on; no other adjustment was necessary. The Rebecca receiver on the aircraft would send out interrogation pulses that then activated the Eureka beacon's signal, which would act as a homing guide at ranges of about 129km (80 miles). This allowed the aircraft to home in with pinpoint accuracy. It was fitted with a demolition charge to ensure it did not fall into enemy hands, although a good number did.

The set itself was reasonably robust; one set was successfully used on seven occasions in Norway despite having been buried for the whole of one summer and a good portion of the winter. Eureka was not that popular with SOE agents, however, mainly due to its bulk and the impossibility of explaining it away if stopped by the enemy. Those who did set up the system found it immensely useful, as the margin of error was a mere 183m (200 yards). That said, many ended up down wells and mineshafts and in rivers. Airborne forces such as the SAS found them invaluable.

## The Drop or Landing

When the aircraft arrived over the drop or landing zone, the standard procedure was to set up the landing lights as follows: three red lights were set about 91m (300ft) apart in line with the wind direction in the centre of a field 609–914m (2000–3000ft) long. A single white light was located 46m (150ft) off to the left of the third red light. The man on the ground operating this light would flash a Morse recognition signal when the aircraft arrived. If Eureka was being used, it should be placed here. If making a parachute drop, the aircraft would approach at 152–182m (500–600ft) along the axis of the lights against the wind as slowly as possible – 160km/h (100mph) for a Halifax.

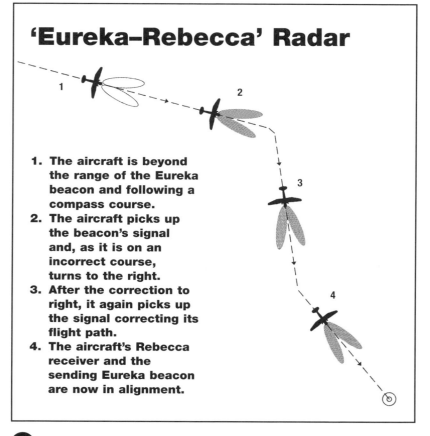

# 'Eureka–Rebecca' Radar

1. **The aircraft is beyond the range of the Eureka beacon and following a compass course.**
2. **The aircraft picks up the beacon's signal and, as it is on an incorrect course, turns to the right.**
3. **After the correction to right, it again picks up the signal correcting its flight path.**
4. **The aircraft's Rebecca receiver and the sending Eureka beacon are now in alignment.**

# Parachutist's Suit

**The Parachutist suit or 'Striptease suit' was designed to be worn over normal civilian clothing and up to two great coats. The suit was packed full of useful pockets and took its nickname from the quick-release zip fasteners that allowed quick egress from the suit.**

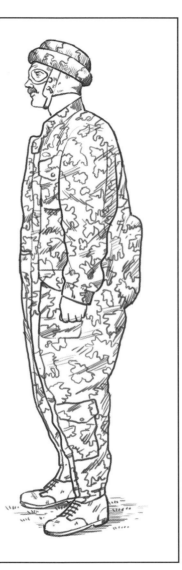

The aircraft then dropped its load over light two.

If it was an agent being dropped, the operative or operatives would have had the opportunity to get some sleep, and were woken before the run-in and given sandwiches and coffee. The dispatcher would then move them forward to get ready to jump. The bombers used by SOE were simply converted by cutting a meter round hole in the fuselage behind the bomb bay and fitting a removal hatch over it. A rail was fitted to which the static line of jumper was clipped. A signal light controlled by the pilot shone red when the drop zone was neared and then green when the first agent was to jump. All he or she had to

# On the Ground

**With a Eureka beacon set up on the ground, a French *Maquis* group receive a new agent freshly landed by Lysander, while other members provide security. The man in a long trench coat, by the plane, conceals the S-Phone used to guide in the aircraft once the Eureka had made initial contact.**

do was step or jump through the hole and the static line would open the canopy.

On the Whitley, the mainstay of SOE operations in the first two years of the war, it was best not to look forward, as the hole was 90cm (3ft) deep and there was every likelihood of receiving a face full of metal. This was known colloquially as 'ringing the bell'. SOE parachute drops were ideally made from 182m (600ft).

This gave the parachute plenty of time to open and in the 10 seconds or so spent in the air the parachutist would have just about enough time to decide whether simply to accept fate and meet the ground rapidly coming towards him; or to attempt

## Equipment Profile:
# The Parachute Landing Fall

The parachute landing fall was (and is) the basic technique for parachutists using round canopy parachutes opened by a static line. SOE used the standard British military parachute, the Type X, which had a silk 8.5m (28ft) diameter canopy designed to allow a descent of 5.1m (17ft) a second. The intention is to distribute and disperse the impact of landing sequentially between five points of contact as the parachutist hits the ground:

1) The balls of the feet.
2) The side of the calf.
3) The side of the thigh.
4) The side of the hip or buttocks.
5) The side of the back.

At about 30m (100ft) above the ground the parachutist needs to look at the ground and determine the direction of drift. At this point the landing position should be assumed. Feet and knees should be pressed together, the knees bent slightly, and the balls of the feet pointed towards the ground. The chin is tucked in and the parachute risers grasped to protect the face and throat. As soon as contact is made with the ground, the jumper should twist the upper body away from the direction of drift, press the outer knee into the inner knee and fall in the direction of drift, taking the impact of landing sequentially on

a simple turn by pulling his lift webs if it was necessary to avoid obstacles or hazards.

If the drop was lower than 182m (600ft), the parachutist was liable to be injured; if it was higher there was a greater possibility of drifting away from the drop zone.

### The Aftermath

This short section is adapted from M.R.D. Foot, *Resistance*, Pierre Lorraine, *Secret Warfare* and James Ladd and Keith Melton, *Clandestine Warfare*:

It is then essential to clear the landing area of any evidence. Although it is good practice to

balls of the feet, the calves, thighs and buttocks. The head should be tucked in tightly to the chest and the neck tensed to prevent the head striking the ground. The jumper should exhale or shout as the upper body hits the ground to reduce internal pressure and help the body absorb the impact. The the jumper should then roll in the direction of drift and release the parachute as quickly as possible to avoid being dragged.

If the landing had gone safely it was then necessary to dispose of the parachute and overalls. Agents would jump in the so-called 'strip-tease suit', a padded camouflaged canvas all-in-one garment, designed to protect the civilian clothing normally worn underneath. The suit had zip fasteners on either side to allow quick and easy removal, hence the name. It also had large pockets that could hold a briefcase, weapons and a folding spade, principally intended for the burying of parachutes.

If the aircraft was landing, the light set-up would be into the wind on a line of two or more lights. It would land by or within 60m (200ft) beyond the first light. The aircraft would then taxi and turn between the last light and its lateral companion, before heading back to the first light, dropping off its cargo and so, facing into the wind, ready to take off again. If a Eureka beacon was used, this would be placed at the first light.

instruct sentries to note the fall of the parachutes, and preferably take a compass bearing or two on the spots were they fell, inevitably some will go astray. The search for canisters must be conducted with discipline and efficiency. The careless smoking of cigarettes and flashing of torches must be avoided when searching for missing canisters. Although H type containers can be broken up into sections for ease of portage, the actual canisters containing equipment and supplies should never be opened on the drop zone. Although there may be a shortage

# How to Land Safely

The parachute landing fall is the standard method of dissipating the impact of a parachute landing. It was taught as part of SOE parachute training and has essentially not changed since.

1. Preparing to land

2. Landing

5. Exhale or shout as the upper body impacts the ground

6. Roll in the direction of the drift

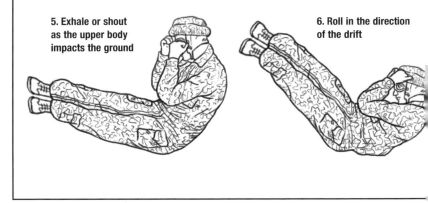

**3. Bend and twist vigorously**

**4. Keep the head tucked into the chest**

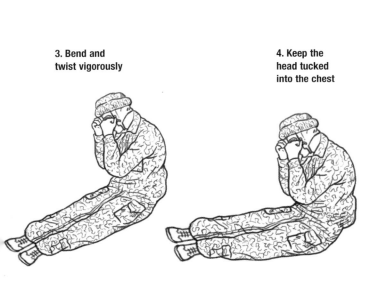

**7. Keep the elbows in and the hands up to protect the face**

**8. Be prepared to disable the parachute so as not to get dragged**

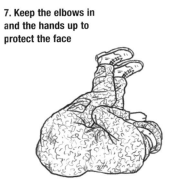

of decent tobacco in the occupied country, opening a canister in the field in search of cigarettes or other 'goodies' is immensely foolish, as the risk of dropping something, such as a clip of ammunition for the Germans to find the following morning, is just not worth taking. Discipline must be maintained under these circumstances. The agent and or equipment should be loaded quickly and efficiently, and spirited away to a secure hiding place as soon as possible. As little a trace as possible should be left behind.

## By Sea

Although inserting agents and supplies by air had a number of advantages, it was not always practicable, due to issues such as aircraft availability, range and weather. There were also advantages. Ships and boats could, generally speaking, carry more, particularly with regard to bulky equipment. Even more esoteric equipment could be transported.

In October 1942 during a joint Royal Navy–SOE attempted attack on the German battleship *Tirpitz*, then berthed at Trondheim in Norway, SOE managed to get two Chariot human torpedoes towed behind a Norwegian fishing boat to within 8km (5 miles) of the target before the operation was abandoned.

Also, at least in the early years of the war, large stretches of the coastlines of occupied Europe were relatively thinly patrolled. The process of landing agents and stores was not all that dissimilar to air dropping materiel in terms of mechanics.

There were, however, difficulties. The enemy operated both sea and air patrols. Hiding a stationary craft amongst the islands of the Aegean or in the islands and skerries of the Leads of the west coast of Norway was reasonably straightforward, but a craft moving during the day leaves a perceptible wake.

Also, very few of the boats available had the speed to operate only at night, given the distances involved in the North Sea and the Mediterranean; and very few of these vessels carried serious anti-aircraft defences.

### Vessels Used

When it came to seagoing craft, SOE was as low a priority as it was with regard to aircraft. Early on in the war, no really fast or sizable craft were available.

The French Section managed to pry a seaplane tender out of the RAF, although, as one who operated her noted, she was 'really too small and slow for the work required of her … her small size was a handicap in that it allowed no room on deck for a rigid boat and the control cabin lacked space for reasonable navigational facilities … her cruising speed under the mist favourable weather conditions was no better than 15

# Mission Profile:
# The 'Shetland Bus'

SOE's Norwegian Section established a seaborne communication link between Shetland and Norway. Officially known as the Norwegian Independent Naval Unit, the 'Shetland Bus' service operated from Scalloway and Lerwick in the Shetland Isles between 1941 and the end of the war. The personnel were recruited from Norwegian fisherman and merchant seamen from Norway's west coast, whose expertise and local knowledge proved vital.

For the first three seasons they used a large number of Norwegian 15.25–21.3m (50–70ft) fishing cutters. Their main business was to take agents in and out and land equipment and supplies in the occupied country. However, a boat captained by Leif 'Shetlands' Larsen, the most decorated Allied seaman of the World War II, towed the Chariot human torpedoes across the North Sea, in the failed SOE–Royal Naval attempt on the German battleship *Tirpitz*. Eight boats and 50 men were lost before three US submarine chasers were received in 1943 and casualties subsequently ceased.

# Seaplane Tender

**The RAF was more sympathetic in the early days of SOE than the Royal Navy and provided a seaplane tender, 360, which undertook some of SOE's seaborne cross-channel operations in the winter of 1941–42.**

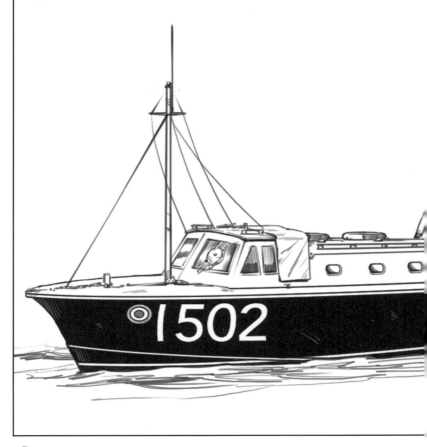

knots. This meant, of course, that she could not operate during the short summer nights.'

That said, her crew carried out at least four successful operations in the winter of 1941–42. SOE managed to get hold of three Brittany fishing boats, a tunnyman, a long-liner and a motor trawler. These could hold 5 tons of stores or more but could only make 7–8 knots. Five more fishing boats were obtained over the course of the war.

In the mid-winter of 1943–44, SOE received three 28-ton Motor Torpedo Boats (MTBs) and two Motor Gun Boats (MGBs) from the Admiralty. These were fast, cruising at 21 knots, and capable of 27 knots in extremis. They packed serious firepower too.

The MGBs were armed with one 57mm (2.2in) 6-pounder and one 40mm (1.57in) 2-pounder guns, twin 20mm (0.79in) cannon and two twin 12.7mm (0.5in) and two 7.7mm (0.303in) machine-guns.

They also carried a 4.3m (14ft) surf boat, which was almost invisible, thanks to its special camouflage. However, these MTBs and MGBs could only carry about 2 tons of stores apiece. They were based on the Helford River, just west of Falmouth on the south Cornish coast.

Similarly, the SOE Norwegian Section operated a service across the North Sea out of Lerwick in the Shetland Islands, the so-called 'Shetland Bus' using Norwegian

# HMS *Fidelity*

**HMS *Fidelity* was a converted, heavily armed merchantman that undertook a number of special agent landing missions in France before being sunk in December 1942.**

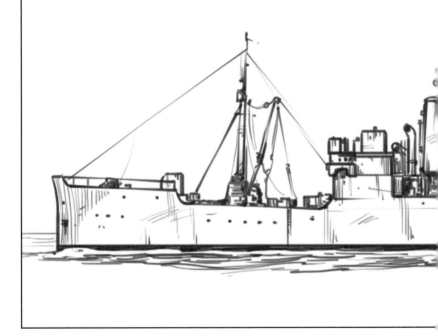

fishing boats and whalers. Eight were lost before they were replaced by three American 33.5m (110ft) submarine chasers, capable of 22 knots. There were no more loses thereafter. In the calmer waters of

the Mediterranean there was plenty of scope for small boat operations. HMS *Fidelity*, a 2400-ton, heavily armed converted merchantman operating out of Gibraltar, was used to drop agents on occasion

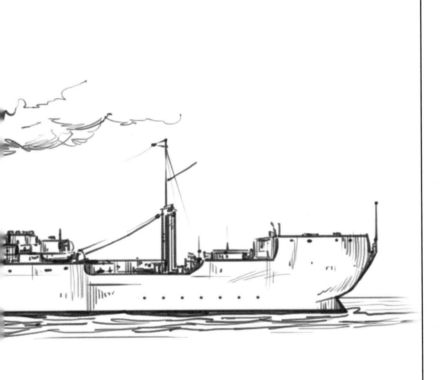

before being sunk in December 1942. SOE also operated a number of 20-ton fellucas, the traditional eastern Mediterranean sailing boats.

A French submarine, the Casabianca, made fairly regular trips to the southern French coastline, often carrying SOE agents. This rather raises the question as to why submarines, an obvious choice for such secretive work, were not used more often. Largely this was down to

Admiralty reluctance to risk such valuable craft, and they certainly were not designed specifically for the purpose. Nonetheless, they were used on occasion both by SOE and the Combined Operations organization's commandos.

### The Welman and Welfreighter

SOE even designed its own one-man midget submarine the Welman, for penetrating enemy harbours. The 2086kg (4600lb) submarine's controls were 'as simple as those in a modern motor car'. It had a 'reasonable range' of about 53km (33 miles) (it would be towed to within range of the target by boat or submarine) and in the view of SOE 'compared to the canoe, the Welman has obvious advantages as it is mechanically propelled, has a smaller silhouette and can submerge and consequently disappear at will'.

Despite the immense effort put into its development, the Welman was used only once operationally. The attempt to penetrate Bergen

# Welman Submarine

**The Welman submarine was developed by SOE as a means of attacking enemy ships in harbour. Although an immense amount of effort was put into the design, their one operational deployment was unsuccessful.**

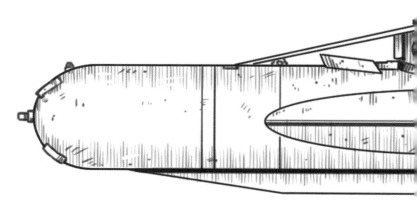

harbour by four Welmans piloted by two Norwegian members of SOE and two Royal Naval personnel in November 1943 was aborted after the capture of Sergeant Bjørn Pedersen by a German patrol vessel.

The Welfreighter was an adaptation of the Welman concept. It was a 13-ton 5 cwt 3–4 man (two crew and up to two passengers) submersible that could carry a ton of stores. However, progress on its development was slow and the war ended before it could be deployed.

## Seaborne Insertions

The following section is adapted from M.R.D. Foot's *Resistance*.

The first thing to consider when planning a seaborne insertion is the impact of such an operation on other agencies. All operations are subject to Royal Navy approval, and the Secret Intelligence Service, given its coast-watching responsibilities with regard to the German Navy, also has a veto.

Consequently, SOE operations are dependent on Admiralty and SIS

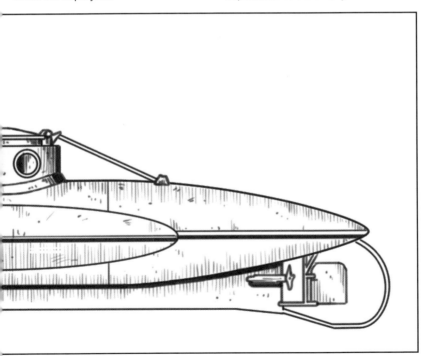

# Welfreighter

**The Welfreighter was a development of the Welman, designed to allow the supply of Resistance groups covertly by sea. The 13-ton design was, however, never used operationally.**

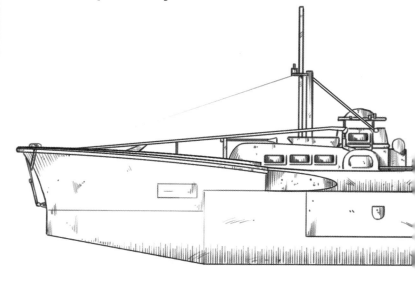

approval. There is a blanket ban on operations on the North French coast east of the Channel Islands.

**Naval Requirements for a Landing Place**
Darkness and reasonably calm water are essential, as is freedom from off-shore reefs and shoals. This can

be determined by consulting the relative map or chart, aerial photographs and consulting those with local knowledge. Generally speaking, it is inadvisable to make landings close to an enemy naval installation, coast battery or any other defensive installation. That said,

such a fool as to attempt to land under their very noses. My best beach was within 12m (40ft) of an occupied German pill-box, this beach was used on six occasions.' The organiser must use his common sense.

For navigation and the proper identification of the beach, it is necessary that there be some nearby landmark or distinctive object visible from low down offshore. Possible landmarks might be a headland, church tower, or even an isolated building. The more steep-to the beach, the easier it will be to use, whatever the state of tide and the more sheltered it is from the prevailing winds, the more often it will be free of surf.

### Preparations Prior to Sailing

The agents to be landed will assemble for a final briefing in London and are then driven down with the conducting officer to one of the several hotels used in the Torquay area. The usual cover is of commandos on leave. The operation will be undertaken on a moonless night.

Once the Admiralty's Deputy Director, Operations Division (Irregular) and the naval Commander-in-Chief Plymouth have all given approval for the operation to sail, the agents should embark in uniform during normal naval visiting hours (noon to 1400 hours) on the Depot ship of the 15th MGB Flotilla at

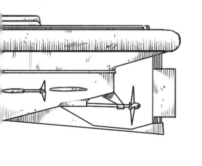

Captain Peter Harratt, responsible the French Section's seaborne operations reckons that 'the best landing points are near a German pill-box, as the garrison of these, knowing as they do that their opponents have photographed the coast, do not expect anyone to be

Falmouth. They should stay below decks. Five minutes before sailing they will be unobtrusively transhipped to the vessel that will take them to France. Before leaving, a careful check should be made of the agent

or agents to make sure they 'neither rattle nor shine'.

**Departure, Sailing and Landing**
The BBC will confirm with the reception committee whether the

# SC-497 Class Submarine Chaser

**The deployment of SC 497 Sub Chaser by SOE's Norwegian Naval Section was a leap in capability in terms of both speed and firepower. The losses that had blighted the section ceased after its deployment.**

operation is to go ahead or not. Plymouth Command will have cancelled its normal nightly anti-E-Boat (German torpedo boats) sweep and the RAF will provide fighter cover in daylight hours. The time of departure should be planned to ensure that the craft will not arrive within 48km (30 miles) of the enemy coast until two hours after sunset. Once the 48km (30-mile) point is reached, the silencers will be turned

on to the engines and the speed reduced. At about 24km(15 miles) from the coast, the main engines will be cut and the journey continued on the auxiliaries in complete silence, at a maximum speed of about 6 knots. This will reduce the wash and consequent phosphorescence.

Once close inshore, the exact drill must be followed. No lights should be shown at sea. There will be no smoking or talking on deck. Contact will usually be made by S-Phone. Failing that, the receiving party will flash a letter in Morse by torch. Once the MGB is satisfied with the signal, it will anchor off shore and the landing party should board the surf boat. A naval rating will stand by to cut the anchor rope in case of emergency. The landing party in the surf boat will row in with muffled oars. The officer-in-charge will go ahead to verify the reception committee's bona fides. Only then will the agents be carried ashore by the crew to avoid getting them unnecessarily wet. They should wear the gas capes provided by the sailors to protect their clothes. Once on the beach, the agents should be as unobtrusive as possible. While waiting they should sit, apart from during first disembarkation when they should stand by the boats. They should never communicate with the outgoing party or talk among themselves. Headgear should not be worn, lest it is lost and leave a trace of the landing.

The party should anticipate the MGB being at anchor for about an hour and a half and plan accordingly. However, turnarounds of 35 minutes have been achieved and conversely the process has taken three and half hours, although that was due to the rowing party getting in lost in fog. Actual time spent on the beach should not be more than three or four minutes. The landing should be made on a rising tide to cover any footprints made in the sand. A member of the reception party should return at first light to ensure no suspicious traces are evident. A nearby safe house is an advantage, but not indispensible: the agents are young and fit. After feeding and resting, they should be sent on their way by mid-day at the latest.'

## By Land

SOE ran a number of land routes into occupied Europe; or rather most of them led out of Nazi-controlled territory, at least in the early years. Valuable personnel, such as shot-down airmen needed to be returned to duty, while agents often withdrew along these well-organized escape routes. There were lines over the Pyrenees from France into Spain and into Switzerland, and from Norway into Sweden, but the circumstances in these neutral countries precluded major traffic going the other way. Once Allied forces returned to Italy, communication lines were established between the partisans fighting in the north and liberated territory in the south, although air drops remained the preferred method of supply.

Yet for the Soviets in the aftermath of the German invasion of 22 June 1941, there was always a land frontier between German-occupied territory and areas still in Soviet hands. With vast numbers of Red Army troops trapped behind the advancing German Army, organizing and equipping Partisan bands required outside support and guidance. The Partisan Movement involved perhaps a million fighters, although never more than 250,000 active at one time, and caused the Germans considerable difficulties behind their lines. So, it is worth turning to the Soviet Partisans when considering movement through the enemy front line and into their rear areas.

The following section is adapted from Lester Grau and Michael Gress (eds), *The Partisan's Companion, 1942: The Red Army's Do-it-Yourself-Guide, Nazi-Bashing Guerrilla Warfare Manual*.

## Crossing the Front Line

Crossing the front line requires careful and meticulous preparation. You should liaise with the local Red Army commander to ensure local friendly forces are aware of your move. Systematic reconnaissance of the enemy is also essential. You must have a complete picture of his locations, flanks, unit boundaries, the location of his weapon systems and any obstacles, such as minefields.

It is also necessary to be familiar with the region in which you will be operating. Study maps and talk to any available locals. Know where the forests, open and broken terrain, gullies, rivers and bridges and population centres are. If possible, use knowledgeable guides who know the area and have connections with the local population. This preparation will allow you to choose the best location to cross the front line.

### Avoiding Contact

Do not help the enemy detect your crossing. Check weapons and equipment to ensure that nothing is loose and rattles or might reflect light. To ensure security do not take documents, photographs or personal letters across. It is best to cross in poor weather. Fog, rain, strong winds (blowing towards you from the enemy's side) snow and blizzards are the Partisan's friends. The darker the night, the better.

When crossing the front line, avoid any contact with enemy units – skirmishes are to be shunned. Do not stop unless it is a dire emergency and try to clear the tactical depth of the enemy forward lines in a single bound. Once you have reached the planned area of operations, then

# Soviet Partisans

Partisans moving from one area to another would often travel lightly, with the intention of building a new base in their new area of operations. This group of Soviet Partisans carry a mixture of Red Army and German weaponry, incuding the PPSh-41 sub-machine gun and the MP40.

mass forces and begin Partisan action as soon as possible.

A great deal is dependent on the density of the enemy's defences. In unoccupied areas, Partisans can move into the enemy's rear area comparatively easily, if they make proper reconnaissance and take proper security measures. However, usually the situation is more difficult. Therefore, the Partisan may have to crawl from cover to cover.

It may be worth sending some men onto the flanks to create a diversion to draw attention away from the main group. If there is a heavy enemy presence, then the infiltration will have to be done in small groups or even by individuals. Under such circumstances it is extremely important to designate a rallying point beyond the front line.

Be vigilant for enemy firing positions through the depth of the line, as well as enemy reserves, patrols and other security forces. Always be on the lookout for such encounters. Reconnaissance and security measures are your precautions against the unexpected. So take concealment seriously – no smoking, coughing or chatting with comrades. Move carefully and cautiously. Avoid roads – they will be used by the enemy. The enemy may have mined them and also trails. They may have set an ambush near them. When moving by compass or with a guide, never forget to use your

**Partisans would typically dress in a mixture of Red Army uniform (many were soldiers cut off from their units) and civilian clothing.**

# French Resistance – Areas of Activity

**The French Resistance and *Maquis* relied heavily on weapons, explosives and communications equipment supplied by the SOE. The map shows the main areas where air drops were made.**

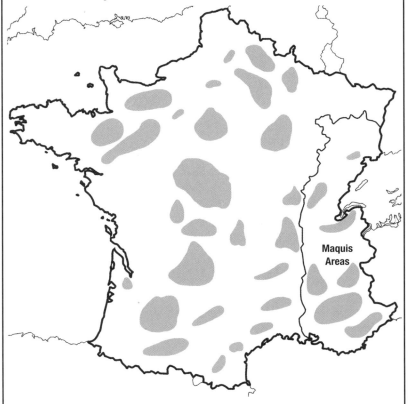

Maquis Areas

hearing as well as sight. Always use darkness to travel through the heaviest density of enemy positions – safer, emptier areas can be moved through at dawn.

## Avoid Occupied Areas

If moving through forested areas, avoid meadows, roads and cuttings. Be careful of lone buildings – they require meticulous reconnaissance. When you are sure the area is clear of the enemy – move forward fast. Always be aware of the possibility of ambush. The Fascists may be concealed in folds in the ground, shell holes, houses and trees. They may well let a Partisan group pass before opening fire from the rear. Remember, the Fascist sub-machine gunners' fire is mostly intended to have an effect on morale. On the whole, losses from this kind of gunfire are slight.

If a Partisan group runs into an ambush, they should drop to the ground. Previously designated troops should attack and kill the ambushers. They must identify the direction of fire and close in by quick bounds. In all cases of sudden encounters with the enemy a quick calculation should be made. Try to determine the enemy's strength and then decide whether to fight and destroy the enemy or escape quickly and change direction. Once the Partisans lose the enemy, they can resume moving towards the correct objective.

## Treatment of Locals

If the Partisans should meet a local inhabitant, it will be necessary to take precautionary measures. If the local has been intercepted by a reconnaissance party and has not seen the main body of the group, he must not be allowed to know either its strength or its direction of movement.

After the main group has passed undetected, the patrol will interrogate and then release the detained local. If he has seen the main body, he must be detained and thoroughly searched and interrogated to determine that he does not belong to the Fascist police or local administration that the Hitlerites install in the captive regions. Any information that he can provide about the enemy will be useful.

In order to hide the true direction of travel from the local, it should be changed. The detained local should accompany the group for a few kilometres and then left behind in the company of a couple of guards until the main body has disappeared. He may then be released and the Partisans will, once again, change direction and move on to the designated area.

While crossing the front line – do not forget to keep your eyes open and conduct reconnaissance for the Red Army. Remember: you are bringing out the most current information about the enemy.

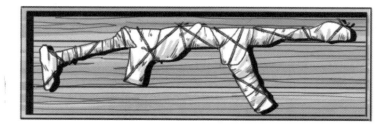

Although the distinction should not be considered uniform, broadly speaking it is possible to divide the resistance campaigns conducted by the various movements supported by SOE, OSS and Soviet Central Staff of the Partisan Movement and the NKVD into two distinct groups.

There were those who operated in urban or at least reasonably populated areas and relied on the existing infrastructure to survive, and then there were those who did not. This did not preclude an operative moving from urban to rural environments and back, however.

There are areas of wilderness in Europe that allowed bands of guerrillas or Partisans, at times, to live, move and congregate in reasonably large numbers. In France, armed resisters, or the *Maquis*, operated in the mountainous areas of Brittany and, famously, in the Vecours region of south-eastern France. Italian Partisans were active in the Apennine Mountains and the Alps.

In Yugoslavia large bands of Chetniks and Communists survived and caused the Germans immense problems. SOE and OSS sent

**Agents, Partisans and Resistance fighters could operate effectively in relatively large groups behind enemy lines if they developed the necessary survival skills.**

**2**

**Operating behind enemy lines requires both evasion and survival skills.**

Behind Enemy Lines

support to all these movements and more. Soviet Partisans operated across the territory occupied by the Germans, and proved to be particularly elusive and effective in large areas of wilderness such as the Pripet Marshes.

Thus, skills for outdoor survival and movement were vital. A good number of SOE, OSS and SAS operators, such as the 'Jedburgh' Teams who were sent into France to support the *Maquis* directly before the Normandy Landings, conducted their war solely in this manner.

## Basic Principles of Guerrilla Warfare

The basic tenets are well laid down by Mao Zedong: 'The whole of art of war is based on deception. If we are ready to attack, we must appear incapable of doing so; if we are close to the enemy we must make him think that we are far away and if we are far away that we are close.' Mao highlights the essential point that one should only fight in favourable circumstances: 'When the enemy advance we should retreat; if he withdraws, we harass him; when he retreats we pursue him; when he is weary, we attack him.'

SOE outlined the basic principles of guerrilla warfare thus:
1) Surprise is key.
2) Never begin an operation unless sure of success. If things begin to go badly, abort.

3) Every operation must be carefully planned. Ensure you have an escape route.
4) Always attack at night.
5) Mobility is vital: know the area, routes and modes of transport.
6) Never stand and fight unless you are in overwhelming strength.
7) Never carry incriminating documents and information.

### Retaining Viability

This short section is adapted from 'The Partisan Leader's Handbook' in *The Secret Agent's Pocket Manual, 1939–45*.

Thus life in the field is almost as much about survival and maintaining the group's viability and combat power as it is undertaking operations.

In the initial stages of a campaign, before the enemy has recognized the threat and organized countermeasures, it may be possible for members of the group to live at home and continue working. The group may only need to gather to undertake an operation. The longer this mode of existence can be maintained, the better. However, if enemy activity increases, it will in all likelihood be necessary to 'go on the run' and survive in the countryside, moving by night and hiding up by day. The recommended number of such a guerrilla band is dependent on the terrain.

In particularly rugged, forested or mountainous terrain, parties of

# Partisan Areas

**Many of Europe's wilderness areas, usually mountainous or forested, allowed the formation of large-scale guerrilla units. Thus the Germans were confronted with sizeable irregular forces in places such as the Alpine areas of Italy and France, Yugoslavia and the Pripet Marshes of Belorussia and the Ukraine.**

# SOE Agent's Equipment

SOE produced a myriad of special devices and tools for its agents. Probably the most important was the radio, but other more aggressive devices such as the silent Welrod pistol, commando knife, explosives and the ubiquitous time pencil fuse were also available.

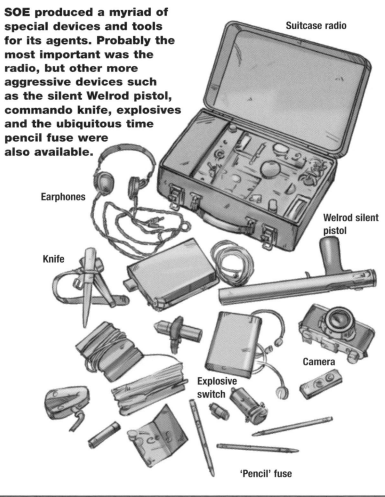

Suitcase radio

Earphones

Welrod silent pistol

Knife

Camera

Explosive switch

'Pencil' fuse

up to a 100 and, in exceptional circumstances, even greater numbers, can survive for long periods. If the countryside is flat, open and heavily populated, even a single man might struggle to remain hidden for an extended period. The more rugged the terrain, the closer the band can be organized, that is, the men can be closely under control at all times and move together to conduct operations or evade the enemy. If conditions are less favourable, the organization must be loser and the group brought together covertly when action is required. If enemy pressure becomes too intense, the group should move and possibly join other parties.

In summary: all actions and sabotage must be swiftly conducted against the enemy in widely distant areas to force him to disperse. These attacks are usually most effective against his communications. This will starve him of supplies and eventually hamper his ability to conduct large operations.

His patrols, sentries and small detachments must be targeted. The aim is to make the whole area unsafe except for large columns. The civilian population is vital for support, supplies and information. You must explain the reason for your actions to the population if they suffer from enemy reprisals. The more effective we are, the more the population will support us, convinced of the enemy's ultimate defeat.

We are fighting for our homeland and families. Our actions aid those fighting the regular war at the front. As we become more effective, so the enemy becomes more ruthless. We must match that ruthlessness, and have greater courage and determination and intensive operations. One must live by the motto 'Shoot, burn and destroy'.

It is worth remembering that regular forces dread guerrilla warfare more than any other form of war. When a guerrilla campaign is conducted by determined men, a successful counter-action by your enemy is almost always doomed to failure.

## Living, Fighting and Surviving in Rural Areas

Based on the experiences they observed in World War II of the *Maquis*, Soviet, Italian, Polish and Yugoslav Partisans and other Resistance movements, the Swiss Army developed a sophisticated guerrilla doctrine. It provides an excellent distillation of the experience of World War II guerrilla movements.

### Formation and Organization of Guerrilla Units

The following section is adapted from H. von Dach Bern's *Total Resistance*.

The enemy will inevitably leave some areas behind the lines sparsely occupied. Guerrilla warfare should be waged away from the front lines.

This is because the enemy is always stronger there and the civilian population will be less supportive. It is also worth noting that frontline troops tend not to engage in repression against the civilian population [it should be noted this was not necessarily the case with regard to the *Wehrmacht*, but as a rule of thumb it holds some merit].

Behind the front the local population will be incensed by the terror tactics used by rear area troops and police, and be more likely to support resistance activities both passively and actively. The enemy is unlikely to use his best frontline fighting units for occupation, security or anti-guerrilla operations; rather, he will initially use second-line troops, which may compensate for your weakness both quantitatively and qualitatively.

In the early stages, when you are organizing your limited resources, you are at your most vulnerable. Therefore, you must not provoke the enemy during this phase. Take the opportunity to equip and stockpile arms. Guerrilla units will require a nucleus of trained troops [also, it should be noted that almost all of continental Europe practised conscription and one of SOE's principal missions was training]. Discover the existing skills of your men and begin training them. Begin to undertake discreet reconnaissance of future targets. Select your leaders

carefully. There is no equivalence to military discipline – no military police, courts martial and state authority – when undertaking guerrilla campaigns. Your troop leaders must be able to handle people. People don't need to make grand military decisions but should have some technical and tactical ability, and be able to conduct small simple operations with competence.

The civilian Resistance movement should conduct sabotage and propaganda operations in heavily occupied zones, while the guerrilla forces should seek to establish liberated areas. These areas should not be held rigidly; if necessary they can be abandoned, for the key rule is 'no terrain is held permanently'. On the whole, these areas can only be held for certain periods, weeks or maybe a month until the enemy decides to act against them and concentrates sufficient forces to undertake large scale counter-guerrilla operations.

Small-scale operations by the civilian Resistance will force the enemy to disperse, while you can retain the initiative. Meanwhile, large concentrations of guerrilla forces can be mustered and can thereby deny the interior to the enemy, forcing him to be satisfied with holding vital points, such as transport routes and communications. He will be unable to establish a reserve and will be forced to disperse his forces to

# Polish Resistance Fighter

Polish Resistance forces were established in November 1939, just a few month after the defeat by Nazi Germany. Originally made up of just 8000 men, by August 1944 it had grown to a force of 20,000 armed fighters for the failed Warsaw Uprising. Polish Resistance fighters were generally armed with a mixture of Polish Army weaponry and captured German arms. This fighter is armed with an MP38 submachine gun, and wears the red and white armband of the Polish Home Army.

# Survival Equipment

**The equipment of Partisans, particularly in the early years, was ad hoc and improvised. It might be stolen from the enemy, requisitioned from the local population or supplied by the government or friendly powers. For survival in winter, decent clothing, shelter and proper cooking equipment were all vital.**

White winter smock

Greatcoat

Tent

Woolly hat

Gloves

Torch

Cooking pot

Stove

# Storage of Weapons and Ammunition

Ammunition should be taken from army caches and enemy dead, and collected in raids on enemy transport and depots. Friendly foreign countries may make systematic air drops of arms, ammunition and equipment. The weapons and ammunition will need to be cached and hidden. As possession of illegal weapons will, more than likely, mean the death penalty, the weapons must be hidden carefully. Burying them is probably the best method.

However, it is important to protect the weapons against damage and rust. Humidity is the major cause of this. Thus the weapons should be completely dry and then covered with a heavy layer of weapons grease (A). Close off the barrel by means of a plug of grease or wax (B). Wrap a rag soaked in grease around the bolt (C). Wrap the entire weapon in a large cloth and secure with string. Place in a wooden box or crate. Wrap the box in tar paper (D). Bury the box in a dry place (E). The best location is within a building, such as a cellar with a gravel floor or barn with a dirt floor.

Check and clean the weapons every two to three months. With regard to ammunition, wrap in each carton or box in about 10 layers of newspaper and place in a box with a layer of two to three inches of sawdust on the bottom. Close and wrap as per weapons. The sawdust will absorb the humidity but must be changed every two or three months too.

As noted, humidity is the major problem for weapons and ammunition so care must be taken in the cache's construction. The munitions must not lie on the floor and air must be allowed to circulate. Air the cache as often as possible.

[Adapted from H. Von Dach Bern's *Total Resistance,* 1965.]

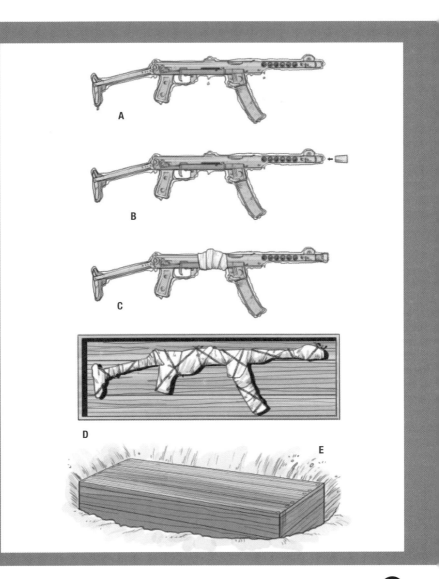

A

B

C

D

E

protect these points, allowing you to retain the initiative. However, if your forces grow too large, you may be tempted to operate openly in a conventional method. It is likely that the enemy will able to concentrate superior forces and destroy you.

# Equipment and Survival

You will almost certainly need to build up supplies of equipment – tents, stoves, torches and warm clothing; snow camouflage can be fashioned from bed sheets. Much of these can be procured from civilian sources. Weapons may be more problematic, and the weapons themselves will be easier to obtain than ammunition. The remaining elements of the Army should be a source of larger weapons. The police may be able to provide small arms. Collect weapons from poorly policed battlefields. Remove weapons from destroyed tanks, fortifications and aircraft. Take weapons from the enemy dead. Farmers, hunters and many families will have privately owned weapons.

## Food Supplies

Food supply raises a number of difficult issues. Guerrilla units should try to live off the land. However, they are often reliant on the civilian population, particularly if operating in 'liberated areas' temporarily under guerrilla control. Friction can very easily arise between the civilian population and the guerrilla units. Food supplies also militate against the permanent establishment of large units – groups of 80–100 can more easily survive than bigger groups. Larger units of, say, battalion size should only come together for larger operations. Non-perishable goods should be hoarded for the winter. Foods with high-calorific content, such as canned milk, chocolate, canned meat and fish, are of particular value.

It may be possible to supplement these by hunting and scavenging. Nonetheless, to feed even small numbers requires the goodwill of the population. Raiding on enemy depots is another, if dangerous, method of finding supplies.

### Underground Storage

The Soviet Partisans reckoned that the best way to store meat and other food supplies was underground. The instructions were straightforward: dig a pit to a depth of about a man's height. It should be shaped like a pitcher, i.e. with a narrower top than bottom. The walls should be lined with straw or reeds held in place by a latticework of sticks. Cover the store with straw, leaves and coniferous tree branches, and finally seal with a layer of dirt. It is worth building a small brush hut above the store to prevent water seeping in when it rains. Such a store is particularly effective in

# Non-Perishable Goods

**Non-perishable food, such as dried beans, smoked or dried fish, canned goods, chocolate and particularly food with high-calorific content, was of particular value to Partisans or agents operating in wilderness areas.**

# Making Underground Storage

**A.** Dig a pit to a depth of a man's height, shaped like a pitcher, i.e. with a narrower top than bottom.

**B.** Line the walls with reeds held in place by a latticework of sticks.

**C.** Cover with straw, leaves or coniferous tree branches, and seal with a layer of dirt.

A

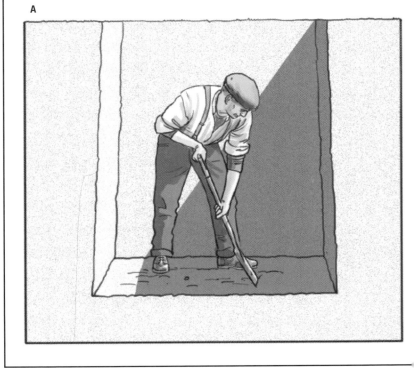

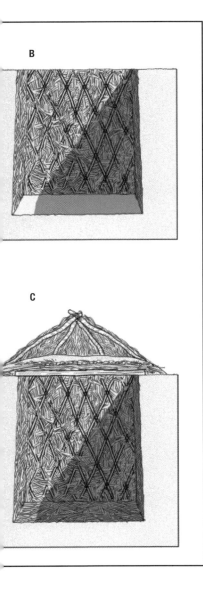

B

C

protecting potatoes from frost.

The Soviets and most Eastern Europeans would have no qualms about collecting berries and particularly mushrooms (one of the Soviet Partisan instruction manuals provides a guide to mushroom picking – given the dangers inherent in that pastime, there is no intention of reproducing it here).

### Freezing Food

Given the temperatures of northern and eastern European winters, the simplest way to preserve meat in winter is to freeze it. Frozen meat should, ideally, be allowed to thaw before cooking. If circumstances require hurried cooking – cut the meat into small pieces without defrosting and put these in a mess tin, with pieces with pork fat and salt. Hang the tin over the fire until the meat is properly cooked. Meat will thaw as the weather warms in the spring. It may spoil and therefore needs to be preserved. It can be dried, cut into strips, sprinkled with salt and put on a tray and baked or roasted in a hot stove. It should remain edible for a decent amount of time.

### Ice Fishing

In the harsh winter, a decent source of protein is frozen fish. By cutting through the ice in lakes and rivers it is often possible to make a very reasonable catch. Many northern peoples eat what is called *strogina*

# Ice Fishing

Ice fishing is a popular pasime in northern European climes. It can also provide a very useful source of protein. A hole is drilled in the ice and the fisherman, using a short light rod and line with bait or lure, aims to catch the fish in the unfrozen water of the lake.

# Mission Profile:
# SOE 'Grouse' Team, Norway 1942–43

The four-man 'Grouse' team from SOE Norwegian Section provided reconnaissance and acted as the reception party for the main assault group on the hydro-electric plant at Vemork near Rjukan in central Norway which was producing heavy water for the German atomic bomb project. They parachuted onto the Hardanger Plateau on 19 October 1942, one of the harshest environments in Europe. They lost much of their equipment and supplies during the drop. The planned landing of a team of British commandos by glider failed a month later and the 'Grouse' party were reduced to eating lichen as a supplement to their meagre rations. They were able to shoot a reindeer just before Christmas which probably ensured their survival. When a second team of Norwegian commandos were parachuted in on 16 February 1943 they were shocked at the state of their colleagues. Nonetheless the joint team successfully assaulted the plant on the night of 27/28 February.

in Russian and considered something of a delicacy. Simply slice fresh frozen fish into very thin strips with a sharp knife. The fish is edible without any further preparation and is highly nutritious.

**Flour from Pine Bark**
In really desperate situations, flour becomes a vital commodity. Anything that can help supplement it is useful. It is possible to make flour from tree bark. This can be used to pad out supplies of normal flour. Pine tree

bark is particularly good. Find a young tree and cut back the outer layer of bark in a strip about a metre wide right round the tree, leaving the inner layer intact. Then, make several vertical cuts and carefully peel off the inner bark with a sharp knife. These should be cut into smaller pieces, then boiled or roasted. Once dry, it can be ground into flour. Birch bark is usable too.

The pine flour can be mixed with rye flour at the proportion 1:3 or even 1:1. If necessary, it can be used on its own. Make dough by mixing it with water or sour milk. Roll the dough thinly, cut into flat breads and bake. They should be perfectly edible and nutritious.

Pine and seed cones held above a fire should open. The seeds are edible. Some lichen are edible [see

*Mission Profile: SOE 'Grouse' Team, Norway 1942–43,* p83]. The best is Icelandic or Reindeer moss. This is grey-blue, tastes bitter and should be immersed in water mixed with campfire ash for some hours, then washed with clean water. It can be boiled to make an edible jelly. If the

# Making Flour from Pine Bark

**A.** Cut back the outer layer of bark with a sharp knife.

**B.** Cut the inner bark into strips.

**C.** Peel away the inner bark.

**D.** Cut the strips into smaller pieces, then boil or roast.

**E.** Pound the roasted bark into a flour.

**F.** Make a dough by mixing it with milk.

**G.** Roll the dough out into flat bread.

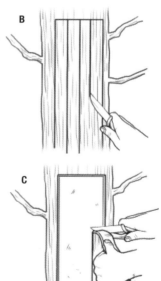

worst comes to the worst it can be soaked in water and eaten raw. Yellow-coloured lichens should, however, always be avoided, as they are poisonous.

**Competing with the Local Populace**

It is worth noting that forcing guerrillas and Partisans to compete with the civilian population is a common tactic of the security forces. Much depends on the ruthlessness of the Partisans; after all, they are usually the ones with guns, but as Mao Zedong recognized, the population's support is vital. Without

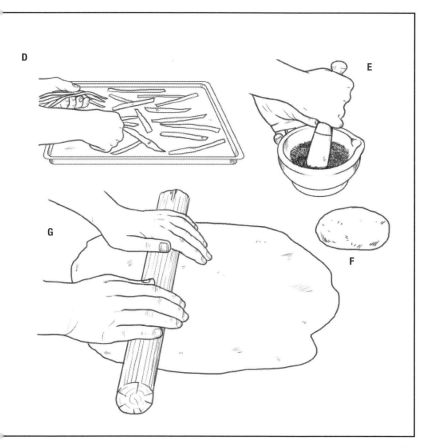

# The 24-Hour Commando Ration Pack

These were issued to troops on D-Day and often supplied to SOE agents parachuted into a wilderness area. The pack contained:

1 tin of a Spam-like product.
1 pack of Biscuits, Plain (hard bread/crackers).
1 block of Chocolate, Vitamin Fortified.
1 sachet of Boiled Sweets.
2 Tea Blocks (late war, Tea-Milk-Sugar combo).
1 pack of Biscuits, Sweet.
1 pack of plain matches.
1 pack of toilet paper.
1 pack of Oatmeal, Instant.
2 packets of Meat Broth.
2 packs of Chewing Gum.
1 pack of Sugar Tablets.
1 Instruction and Menu Sheet.

their sympathy, the guerrilla groups would be unlikely to survive for any length of time. All guerrilla manuals warned against alienating the civilian population through brutality and lack of discipline. It was essential not to become a greater evil than the enemy occupation forces.

The advice was straightforward: don't force the population to hand over something while staring down the barrel of a sub-machine gun; appeal to the common cause and patriotism to gain their help.

## Movement and Shelter

By following such tenets, resistance groups managed to establish themselves, organize and build up weapons and food stocks, and survive in many of Europe's rural areas. Eventually, many would establish 'liberated areas' and operate fairly openly (see *Mission Profile: Yugoslav Guerrilla Band Behind Enemy Lines*, above).

However, large concentrations of resisters tended to provoke an aggressive German response. The

# Mission Profile:
# Yugoslav Guerrilla Band
# Behind Enemy Lines

Major Erik Greenwood, an SOE liaison officer, was dropped into Eastern Serbia in Yugoslavia in April 1943 to provide support and organize operations against German communications along the Danube by General Mihailoviç's Chetnik resistance forces. He was initially most impressed by fact that a whole army could live in enemy-occupied territory. It was broken, heavily wooded terrain that favoured the guerrillas but he thought the survival of a whole army organization 'almost miraculous'.

However, he had real problems in organizing supply drops: the Chetniks used German weapons, so ammunition was often a problem; and his request for uniforms led to an absurdly small and largely useless collection of clothing being dropped. Meanwhile, his exasperation with the Chetniks also increased. He only managed to organize one operation in six months and subsequent reprisals meant his hosts refused to launch another.

Yugoslav Communist Partisans faced seven major Axis offensives between 1941 and 1944 against the areas under their control, including a daring German airborne attempt to capture their leader Josip Broz, better known as Tito, in May 1944.

Broadly speaking, the Partisans met these offensives in a similar manner on each occasion – by resolute resistance (by 1943 Tito had a reasonable artillery park at his disposal) followed by systematic withdrawal once it was clear that they were overmatched. These campaigns were marked by particular brutality, but the Partisans' ability to survive and maintain operational coherence was of particular irritation to the Germans. At times, Tito could muster 250,000 fighters and is credited with holding down some 35 Axis divisions.

In July 1944, in southeast France on the Vecours Plateaux, 4000 *Maquis*, who had been supplied by a number of large-scale air drops, were attacked by some 10,000

# Types of Tracks

Being able to read footprints can give you important clues about pursuers or local civilians.

**A.** Someone running in heavy boots (long strides).

**B.** Someone carrying a heavy load (feet drag between steps).

**C.** Someone wearing heavy military-style boots.

**D.** Stilettoed shoes or boots.

**E.** Someone walking backwards.

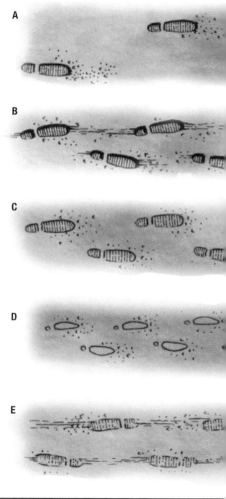

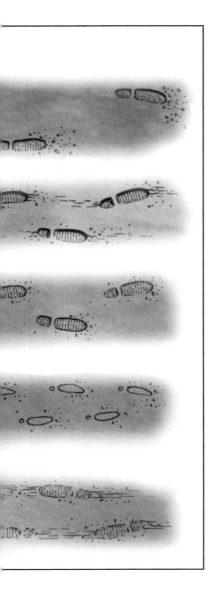

German troops, some landed by glider. The French stood and fought and suffered accordingly. The rural guerrilla or Partisan should rarely attempt to fight conventionally and attempt to hold ground. He should rather rely on guile and stealth. To that end, the ability to move and camp without attracting the attention of the enemy is vital. Soviet Partisans devoted much thought to this.

## Movement

The following section is adapted from Lester Grau and Michael Gress, *The Partisan's Companion, 1942: The Red Army's Do-it-Yourself-Guide, Nazi-Bashing Guerrilla Warfare Manual*.

You must protect your feet – all clothing is important but your boots are the most essential. They should be neither too tight nor loose. Grease your footwear – your boots will be softer and last longer. Wash your feet at every opportunity, as this will prevent blisters and bruises. Cut your toenails short.

The forest provides cover but be careful, especially when approaching the edge, clearings or roads. Always send a three-man scouting party ahead. They should move in single file and remain close enough to be seen by the main party.

A rearguard detachment should also be used. Avoid making noise. Don't break branches or step on dead wood. Don't catch weapons or equipment on trees. Don't talk. Don't drop litter, paper or cigarettes.

If the enemy is near, be especially careful. If walking on grass, put your weight on your whole foot, not just your heel. On hard soil, put your weight on to your toes first, then lower the rest of your foot. On soft soil do the opposite; first put your weight on your heels.

If you are going to sneeze, pinch the bridge of your nose strongly and if this doesn't work, take of your hat and sneeze into that. This also works for coughs.

If moving across large open spaces, only do so at night. Conduct a thorough reconnaissance before moving off. When crossing a road, keep a look-out for patrols and snipers. Try and cross in areas where the forest comes close to the road. In all cases move quickly.

### Crossing Obstacles

If safe to do so, use a ford – a roadway that ends at one side and continues on the other is a sure indication of a safe place to cross. Otherwise, small ripples on the surface of a slow river indicate a shallow spot. If the river has rapids, you might well find a ford below the drops. Marshy areas are rarely suitable. One method for crossing fast-flowing rivers is to stretch a tightrope supported by poles across its width.

# Taking an Indirect Route

**Special forces operatives were taught to take an indirect route, whether when approaching a target or trying to avoid contact with the enemy.**

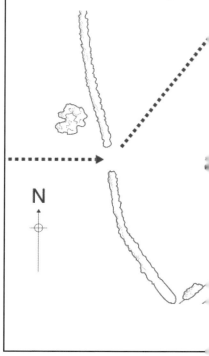

# Equipment Profile:
# Foot Wrappings

The Soviet Army, and before that the Russian Army, eschewed socks in favour of foot wrappings, considering them, at least during World War II, as 'better on the march than socks'. They usually consisted of a square piece of cloth about 40cm x 40cm (16in x 16in), made of flannel for winter use and cotton for the summer. Quite apart from being cheaper and easier to produce and also improvise, the wrappings are arguably more resistant to wear and tear – any holes can be compensated for by changing the wrapping's position. They also dry more quickly than socks. Their main drawback is that, if incorrectly put on, an awkward fold or crease can very easily cause blisters. So the Soviet military authorities issued careful instructions for their use. Under the conditions in the field the wrappings tended to become somewhat malodorous – and plenty of Soviet military humour was devoted to their usefulness as chemical weapons. Nonetheless, they were only phased out by the Russian Army in favour of socks in the late 2000s.

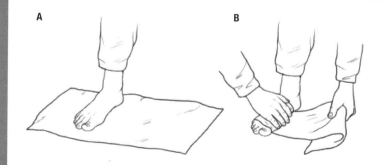

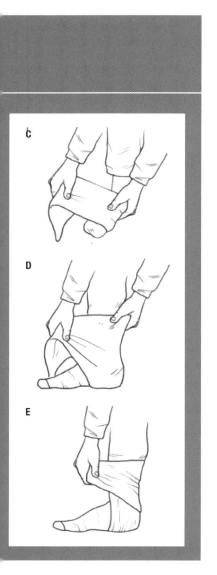

Otherwise, you can cross a river aided by a comrade. Stand face to face with your hands on each other's shoulders and move across. If the river is too deep, it may be necessary to swim across. Remove your boots and wrap them through your belt [Soviet troops tended to wear calf-length leather boots] to prevent water getting inside. Turn out any pockets and unfasten your sleeve and collar buttons. Roll your greatcoat tight and put it across your left shoulder. Put your rifle on top of your tightly packed kitbag, pointing to the right, with the sling across your chest under your armpits.

If possible, use available material such as dry logs, barrels and bails of hay as floats. If you have time and suitable materials make rafts. Tie boards and poles together with rope or wire and reinforce them with floats.

You are especially vulnerable in the water, so enter it quietly. When swimming, do not thrash about and make noise. When you reach the opposite bank, pause and, only when you are sure you haven't been observed, move over the top of the bank find cover.

### Marshes

Crossing marshes requires caution. Local guides may be able to show you routes through. It may be necessary to test the depth and the firmness of the crust. Drop a log into the swamp – if it doesn't sink, step

# Crossing a River

**A man stands more chance of crossing a fast-flowing river if he has a partner to support him. If the river cannot be forded but has to be swum, an improvised float will make the task much easier.**

An effective way to cross a river is for two men to stand face to face, with their hands on each other's shoulders, and slowly walk across

Improvised float

out on to the swamp's top layer near the edge. If it doesn't give way, stamp on it again and again. Then, if it holds, move forward using a pole to probe in front of you.

Step onto bushes and hummocks, as their roots will help support you. If they don't support your weight, build a pathway out of brushwood supported by a layer of poles. If this impossible – lie down and spread your weight and crawl across. One way of doing this is to use two flat boards, putting down one and picking up the one behind and shifting across the

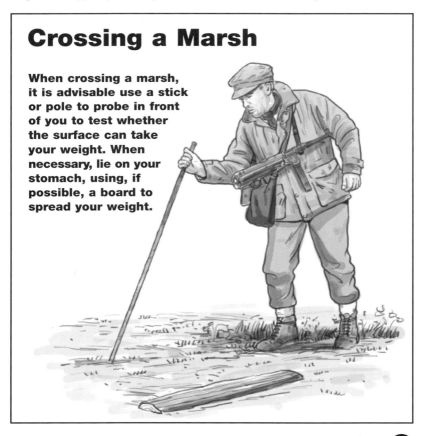

# Crossing a Marsh

**When crossing a marsh, it is advisable use a stick or pole to probe in front of you to test whether the surface can take your weight. When necessary, lie on your stomach, using, if possible, a board to spread your weight.**

marsh. If any one falls into a deep area of quagmire, he should avoid panicking and making frantic movements. Throw him a rope or pass him poles or saplings. Find some firm ground from which to pull him out.

### Drinking Regime on the March
Ensure your canteen is full of water before setting out. It is possible to improvise a canteen if you don't possess one by covering a bottle with cloth and sewing on loops to attach it to your belt.

Do not drink too much too quickly. In the first two or three hours, try to avoid drinking at all. The more you drink, the more you sweat. This will make you thirsty and weaken you. Only drink fully on long halts. When moving, restrict yourself to two or three mouthfuls a time.

[It is worth noting that during World War II the standard practice of most armies was to try to limit water intake to both conserve water and to acclimatize the soldier to less of it. This practice has been discontinued, and since the 1960s armies have encouraged troops to drink as often as possible even when not thirsty – the US Army recommending 1 litre (2 pints) an hour when undertaking any strenuous activity.]

Always refill your canteen at every opportunity, but be careful – not all water is drinkable. Spring water is best and river water can be used. Not all

water from wells is good. If there is a well-beaten path to it, it is likely the water is drinkable. If the well appears abandoned, avoid it.

### Rest and Halts
There two distinct type of breaks on the march: the short halt of 10 minutes after 40–50 minutes; and the long halt of two to three hours after four to five hours on the march. It is worth stopping after a couple of kilometres when you first set out to sort out any problems with clothing, equipment or weapons. It is particularly important to pay attention to any problems with feet or foot wrappings.

On these breaks, take off your greatcoat, put down your weapon and check your foot wrappings, if conditions permit. Lie down if tired and lift your legs and rest them on your kitbag. In winter it will be necessary to take breaks more frequently. If it has snowed, do not lie down in the snow; squat against a tree but do not fall asleep. Before you leave, check that none of your colleagues are napping.

Do not be rigid in your break time-keeping. It may be better to push on another 10–15 minutes to stop in better cover or a place that can more easily be secured.

When taking a long halt in summer, take the opportunity to take off equipment. Wash and dry your foot wrappings. Wash yourself, or if

# Types of Camp Fire

**There are numerous different varieties of campfire. Star fires, for example, give a very controllable heat, while the pit fire are useful for cooking. Long fires and safety night fires are built to prevent the fire accidentally spreading.**

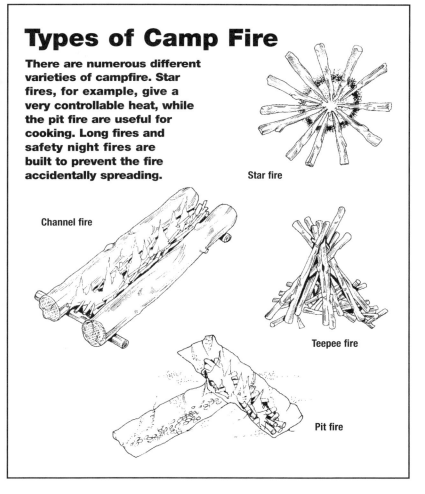

Star fire

Channel fire

Teepee fire

Pit fire

possible take a swim. Stop for the night an hour before nightfall. Ensure the area is safe. Set guards and then prepare for the night bivouac.

## Bivouacs
### Camp fires

If the area is secure, you can light a fire. Do it quickly and easily and make

# Starting a Fire

Matches are a vital commodity. Use them sparingly. Use good kindling such as birch bark, which light even when wet: dry pine and fir sticks and dry lichen help. Dry twigs can be partially shaved with a knife, and tinder such as birch bark, dry grass and small sticks collected and then lit. Matches can get wet, so always keep a few in reserve sealed with a cork in an empty cartridge case. Matches can be waterproofed by being dipped in paraffin. Also, divide the matches up between Partisans and hopefully at least someone's will remain dry.

## Using a Pistol

If matches are unavailable, you can gather kindling as above. Then remove a bullet from its cartridge case and pour some gunpowder on the kindling (A). Loosely plug the cartridge with paper (B) and then fire the cartridge, aiming slightly above the kindling (C). The flash should ignite the dry kindling. Fire can also be started with flint struck against stone or metal to produce sparks.

Always take the opportunity to dry your clothes. this can be done by constructing a drying rack. However, be careful not to place this too close the fire. Be particularly sure not to put wet boots too near, as overheated leather will curl and crack.

sure it is hidden. You should learn how to do this. If the fire is not screened by natural cover, make a screen. In the summer, dig a hole for the fire.

There are a number of types of fire you can make, as time and conditions permit.

- **'Star' fire** – Place the logs as spokes on a wheel pointing towards the centre. Made with thick logs, this will burn long and hot. As the logs burn down, push towards the centre.
- **'Polynesian' Fire** – Set in a shallow pit with the logs standing. This fire does not require much fuel but provides a lot of heat and coals, which are useful for cooking.
- **'Hunter's' fire** – Place three logs, fan-like, on top of two others. Light

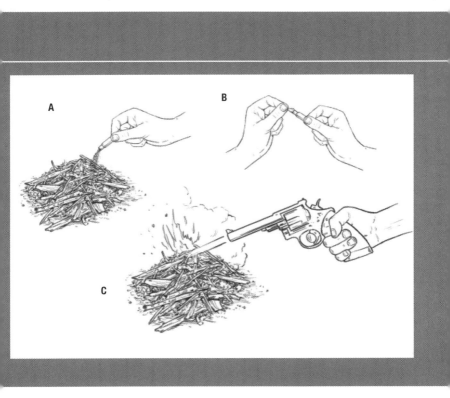

the fire under the upper logs where they cross the lower logs. This burns slowly, providing good heat.

- **'Night' fire** – To hide a fire at night, take two logs and cut a lengthwise channel in each. Fill one channel with hot coals, and place a second log on top, channel side down. The coals and logs burn long and slowly due to the lack of oxygen. The fire should not be visible at more than a few metres away.

- **Pit fire** – Another method is to dig a pit and start a fire in it. Create a chimney with birch bark and sticks to funnel smoke out the pit.

### Shelter

Tents will not always be available, in which case improvised shelters

# Bow and Drill Fire

**A bow and drill system works best with woods such as willow, larch, cedar, poplar, sycamore and mulberry. Avoid woods that are very hard or very soft.**

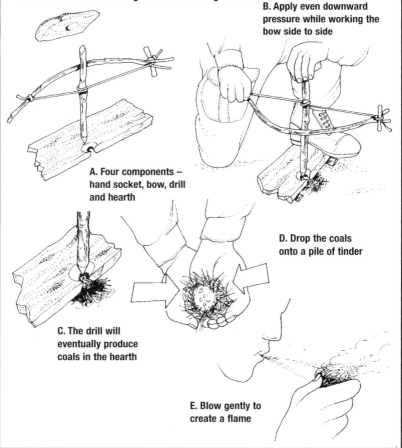

B. Apply even downward pressure while working the bow side to side

A. Four components – hand socket, bow, drill and hearth

D. Drop the coals onto a pile of tinder

C. The drill will eventually produce coals in the hearth

E. Blow gently to create a flame

# Pit Fire

**The pit fire is a classic soldier's campfire. Air flow to the fire is provided via a U-shaped vent dug into the soil – restricting or widening this vent will reduce or increase the heat respectively. Wrapped parcels of food can be placed in the pit for roasting, while the opening above can be used for grilling, boiling and drying.**

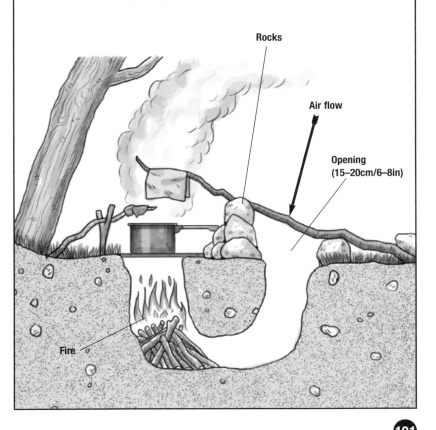

Rocks

Air flow

Opening
(15–20cm/6–8in)

Fire

such as lean-tos [*zaslon* in Russian] should be used. This is a screen built at angle facing the fire at a distance of four or five paces. The screen is built of poles, branches and brushwood or, if convenient, between two trees. During winter, ski-poles can be used instead. Tilt the screen

# Lean-To with Screen

**Here we see a simple lean-to shelter. The frame is built against a frontal weight-bearing crossbeam, supported between two upright posts (or the fork in a tree, as seen here). Cover the frame with thick layers of leaves and foliage, and build a fire reflector in front to push back the heat from your campfire.**

towards the fire to catch the heat more efficiently. Check the wind and make sure that it does not blow the smoke of the fire onto you.

**Lean-To**

In heavy woodland, a simple hut [*shalash*] can built from branches. Simply clear the area and build a

# Round Hut

**The round hut, or in Russian 'Choom', is modelled on the temporary dwellings of nomadic reindeer herders in Siberia. Based on a conical frame of branches, it could be covered with vegetation, skins or canvas.**

small horseshoe-shaped bank. Brace two poles in the banks and tie together. Insert branches or skis into the walls supported by a framework of poles. Cover with spruce branches. Build the fire in front of the entrance and sleep in the hut, with your feet facing the fire. Line the floor with metre-long (3ft) sticks and cover with spruce branches. Use your kitbag as a pillow.

## Round Hut

If more time is available, or more comfort or warmth required, or you are considering staying somewhere for longer than a single night, a more permanent structure can be built. The round hut [*choom*] of about 6m [19ft 8in] diameter can sleep 20 Partisans. It is made of poles 4–5m [13–16ft ]long.

First, make a tripod of the poles and tie their tops together with cord. Then, support 30 or so poles on the tripod with their bases about half a metre (1.5ft) apart. This should produce a conical frame. Interlock the frame horizontally with branches. Cover with coniferous branches and, to aid insulation, throw some snow on these. There should be hole in the top to act as a chimney. A firepit should be dug in the centre of the floor. Dig an air intake from outside into the firepit, and roof with branches.

Line the floor with spruce branches. If it is possible, build the choom over a dugout. This will increase headroom and improve insulation.

## Dugouts

Indeed, dugouts [*zemlianki*] can provide the basis for buildings of considerable durability. At its most basic, a dugout is a large pit with a wooden frame with an overhead cover above it. A layer of dirt can be placed on top. However, these can be quite sophisticated structures. Thick logs should be placed in the pit's walls. These will support the rafters, which will create the gable roof. The rafters are covered with layers of branches, brushwood and dirt. A layer of clay will waterproof the structure. A six-man dugout should be of the following dimensions: 1.8m [5ft 10in] high, 3.2m [10ft 6in] wide and 4m [13ft 1in] long. Make steps down to the entrance and make a door out of some tent canvas or tarpaulin. A partisan dugout needs a second, emergency exit in case of attack. Create a 50cm x 50cm [19.5in x 19.5in] window at the back end to serve as this exit. If glass is not available, tar paper can be used. The dugout should be heated by a stove with a chimney funnelled through the roof.

# Hardships of Partisan Warfare

The Soviet Partisan movement illustrated the difficulties of conducting a dual struggle for survival, against both the Germans and the elements. Procuring food, clothing, arms and equipment was a constant challenge. It was an isolated and precarious existence. Stalin made it clear that the Partisans – at least in the early years – could not depend on the support of the state. They were to acquire weapons and provisions from the enemy. Thus, in day-to-day terms, the most daunting task was simply to survive, particularly as units expanded,

# Building a *Zemlianki*

**These shelters, based around a dugout with a wooden frame and overhead cover, provided essential shelter for many of Eastern Europe's Partisans when they were living in more permanent camps.**

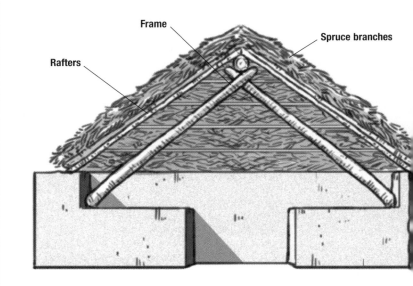

Frame

Spruce branches

Rafters

reaching in some cases hundreds and even thousands of men and women (see *Operative Profile: Tuvia Belski,* page 109).

On top of this, the German occupiers had denuded the Russian country by harsh requisitions, the

Soviet military had conducted a scorched-earth policy as it retreated, and the reduced rural population meant there were fewer people available to work the land. Large areas of the Soviet Union were on the verge of, or actually suffering, famine. Consequently, rations were often short and monotonous, and on many occasions Partisans were forced to survive off forage. Outbreaks of scurvy and dysentery were brought on by eating grass and nettles and such like. So many members of a Partisan Brigade in the Orel had stomach complaints from such a diet that their commander forbade the consumption of grasses and flowers. On top this, the brigade was suffering from 168 cases of typhus out of 1089 personnel.

The diet and conditions in the forest led also to skin conditions, dental problems and more serious illness such as malaria and tuberculosis. In times of extremis, such as in the Crimea in the winter of 1942–43, Partisans starved to death and even resorted to cannibalism.

The warmer months were hardly bucolic. Spring brought melting snow, and autumn rains brought on the *rasputitsa*, the all-engulfing mud that brought virtually everything to a halt. Just to add to the Partisans' misery, there was an issue not seriously addressed in their manuals – the prevalence of the mosquito. In the summer months, plagues of

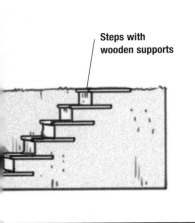

**Steps with wooden supports**

# Snow Tree Shelter

A snow tree shelter takes advantage of the fact that the branches of a pine tree provide a natural and dense form of overhead shelter. Dig out the snow from around the base of the tree and line the floor with thick layers of foliage. With you hunkered down beneath, the low-hanging branches above you will provide some degree of waterproof and windproof protection.

mosquitoes, particularly in swampy areas, attacked any exposed area of flesh. One group in Briansk was driven by mosquitoes from their forest camp to a local village, where they were promptly destroyed by the Germans.

The harshness of the winter, quite apart from increasing food scarcity, required decent warm clothing, which was inevitably in short supply. Survival also required shelter, particularly after the terrible winter of 1941–42. While sleeping under the stars in the summer or in bivouacs for a single night in harsher times was possible, more permanent structures were required for long-term survival. So the Partisans constructed often quite sophisticated *zemlianki* or dugouts, which were often excellently camouflaged. Indeed, some larger groups created bases with dugouts and even buildings housing workshops, cookhouses, hospitals and washing facilities.

That said, more mobile groups had no such luxuries, which it must be said is a very relative term. In spite of these conditions and the morale-sapping nature of day-to-day existence, the Soviet Partisans endured and survived. On top of this, they continued to take the fight to the Germans and had a real strategic effect on the war on the Eastern Front. This is a tribute to Soviet Partisan doctrine and the survival skills it outlined, but especially to the

## Operative Profile: Tuvia Belski (1906–87)

Tuvia Belski grew up in the part of Eastern Poland seized by the Soviets in 1939. In the aftermath the German invasion of the Soviet Union he began to organize a Jewish resistance group. In the Naliboka Forest he established a functioning community with a school, hospital and nursery which would grow to 1200 people. Although mainly concerned with saving Jewish lives, Belski claimed to be the 'commander of the Soviet company of Partisans named for Marshal Zhukov' and his group cooperated with mainstream Russian partisan units on many occasions. It was the largest Jewish partisan group, surviving for over two years in the forest.

determination and courage of the Partisans and the civilian population that supported them in the face of a brutal and remorseless enemy.

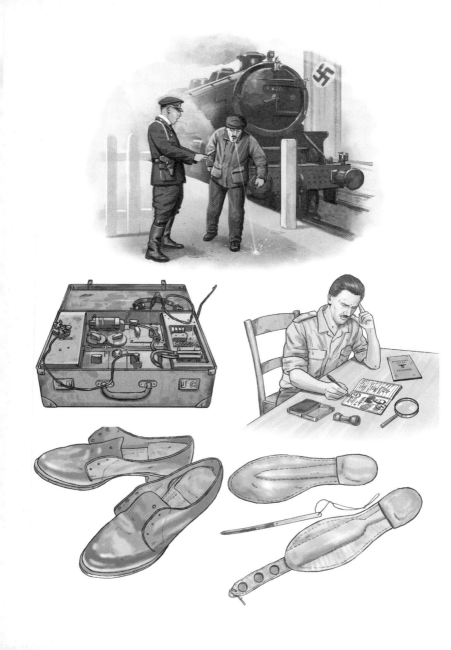

The Nazi centres of power in occupied Europe inevitably resided in the capital cities. The bureaucratic heart of modern society, the civil service, police, radio stations and communications hubs, were located there.

A very large proportion of the population lived in urban areas. If the Allied saboteur or agent was to gain information, sow discord and strike against the occupiers, he or she inevitably had to operate in cities and towns. This required a particular set of skills, some of which overlapped with the urban operative's rural partisan or guerrilla counterpart.

Combat skills were equally useful wherever the agent worked, although concealable weapons such as the pistol and sub-machine gun would be preferred to longer-ranged weapons such as the rifle. Radio operators had to be particularly careful about giving away their location.

Yet organizing and operating in towns and cities, working and living unobtrusively amongst the civilian population, often cheek by jowl with the police and the occuping forces, required some quite specific skills and techniques.

••••••••••••••••••••••••••••••••

**Clandestine Resistance fighters and agents used many specialist devices and equipment to carry out observation, intelligence and sabotage activities.**

# 3

**Operating in the urban environment, often at the heart of enemy-occupied territory, required a particular set of skills, and particular character and nerve.**

# Working Under Cover

# Leather Travel Case

**A leather case designed to hold a complete toilet set can be a very useful place for concealing messages, microfilm and money. The case includes a number of built-in hiding places, as well as items such as a hollow shaving brush and hairbrush with a false back.**

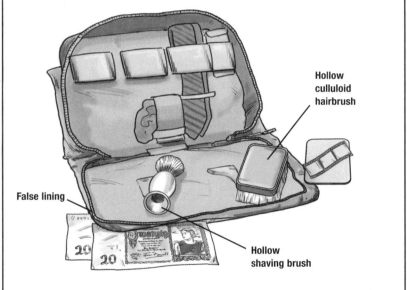

Hollow culluloid hairbrush

False lining

Hollow shaving brush

## The Skills of Clandestine Living

As part of their overall training SOE agents undertook a three-week course in clandestine living, involving classes on the skills and techniques this required, the enemy's security apparatus, on propaganda and on coding. They were advised to proceed slowly and cautiously when they arrived in occupied territory and find an inconspicuous medium-sized hotel. They were more likely to attract attention in more intimate lodgings such as small guesthouses or hostels. Apparently setting oneself up in a brothel was ill advised, as prostitutes were often used as police informers in continental Europe. It was necessary for the agent to stay alert, ensure that his or her papers were in order, remember the cover story, be discreet and keep quiet.

Police, when conducting routine business, are always on the look-out for anything unusual. SOE agents were advised to 'be average' in terms of dress and behaviour (although see *Operative Profile: Denis Rake*, page 114, for a notable exception). They should shun the limelight and certainly not drink too much or womanize.

### Establishing a Cover Story

It was always necessary to have a good cover story. As part of the

# Answering Routine Questions

A sensible operator was encouraged to constantly run through their mind the answers to routine questions they were likely to be confronted with at a checkpoint or a police spot check, such as 'Who are you?', 'Where are you?' – this could be a bit awkward for an agent fresh from a parachute drop – 'Where are you going and why?' 'Where do you live?''

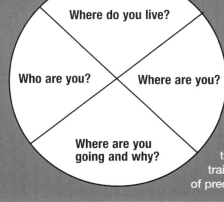

**Where do you live?**

**Who are you?**

**Where are you?**

**Where are you going and why?**

A policeman might ask two or three of these sorts of questions to reassure himself of the agent's bona fides. If it was seven or eight, the agent ought to be worried as the policeman surely had some suspicions. As the manual said, security 'is a frame of mind attainable through self-discipline and self-training that will make the taking of precautions a "habit"'.

# Operative Profile:
# Denis Rake (1901–76)

Denis Rake joined SOE in 1941 after serving as a translator in the Army during the French campaign of 1940. He had grown up in Belgium, hence his excellent language skills, and had worked in the theatre. When, in early 1942, he was forced to flee from Lyon, he took refuge in Paris, where his pre-war theatrical contacts came in useful. However, in the face of just about every rule of security, he took up with a German officer he met in a bar, convincing him that he was a Belgian cabaret artist looking for work. Apparently during their fairly brief affair, the German officer never suspected that his lover, who began performing in drag at a number of Parisian nightclubs, was a British agent. He was later captured – nothing to do with his period in Paris – and, despite being terribly injured during torture, escaped and managed to get across the Pyrenees to neutral Spain.

preparation for the mission the agent and his or her SOE handler would prepare a back story for the field. There were a number of approaches. The agent could base the story on their own, indeed use their own identity. Clearly, it had the advantage of being largely true, easy to remember and backed up by records. There would be gaps, but these could be reasonably easily filled. However, it was possible the enemy would be aware of previous subversive activity.

They could also use someone else's identity. Again, there would be an existing record but there was the possibility of meeting one of the original person's acquaintances. The use of a fictitious identity avoided the possibility of any entanglements but there would be no trace of the person in official records.

It was ill advised to adopt more than one identity due to the possibilities of self-contradiction and of being caught in possession of two identity cards. The SOE training syllabus set a list of things to consider when establishing a cover story. It needed to be plausible and obviously not link you to previous subversive activity. It was better to base it on the facts of the agent's life. The agent should never include places and people he did not know, nor should he claim any skills or occupation which he could not substantiate. People who were not engineers should not claim to be an engineer. It was particularly important to be able to back up any details on the identity papers. The agent's most recent history would particularly interest the police, and it was also the most difficult to fabricate, given the agent had most likely spent the time in a SOE training school. The forged documents issued were of the

# Creating Forged Documents

**SOE and OSS assembled teams of forgers and draftsman to create painstaking facsimiles of official German documents and passes. This could be the well-regulated process undertaken at Station XIV near Royden in Essex in the United Kingdom. In field offices operating in, say, liberated Italy, the creation of forged papers might be a more improvised, if no less painstaking, affair.**

# Establishing a False Identity

Once the agent arrived it was important to start establishing the false identity. It was important to visit places that they claimed to have been to and make acquaintances in the area. All of this would give the cover story weight and substance. The SOE syllabus listed the basic procedures to protect the agent's cover:

*Name: Always respond to it immediately and be able to sign it without thinking.*

*Consistency in general: your personality and conduct must fit your cover.*

*Expenditure should meet ostensible income.*

*Documents and clothes should be suitable.*

*Knowledge, education, accent, manners and taste should fit.*

*Character of friends and acquaintances should be appropriate to background.*

*Avoid slang that has developed amongst the exile community in Britain.*

highest quality, but it was necessary to know how they would have been issued legally. It was important not to carry anything that did not fit in with the cover story, although conversely things like unofficial papers, tickets and the like could support it.

## Understanding Local Conditions

It was also necessary to get a feel for the situation that the agent had been sent back into after months, possibly years, away. It was vital to know what was off limits due to

*Avoid customs and knowledge that might have been acquired in Britain and adapt to new customs and language that have arisen in your country in which you are operating.*

*Cover occupation: A cover occupation will provide you with a reason for being in the area, explain your income and hopefully avoid German labour conscription. A real job is best, but your subversive work might preclude this. However, it is helpful to have a real employer to vouch for you.*

*Unregistered jobs such as student and stamp dealers are a possibility. Remember that some occupations have specific restrictions on liberty or specific investigation of credentials. The job also needs to be compatible with your cover, support your movements and access to transport. Always ensure that you have adequate qualifications for the job selected.*

*Conclusion: A good cover is hard to establish and easily destroyed. Nonetheless serious investigation of your cover is likely to expose its flaws. Therefore, always ensure you do not that attract the attention of the authorities.*

[Adapted from the SOE syllabus, 'Cover: November 1943' in *How to be a Spy: The SOE Training Manuals.*]

shortages and rationing, so as not to order the wrong drink or cigarettes, for example, and so attract unwanted attention. Indeed, Evangeline Bell, who processed US Office of Strategic Services (OSS) agents for the field, recalled that agents being sent to France were taught to smoke their cigarettes right down to the stub. Apparently, one had been captured by the Gestapo because he tossed away a half-smoked cigarette, something a frugal *paysan* or countryman would never do in tobacco-starved France.

A knowledge of the black-out regulations, curfews and travel restrictions had to be gained quickly. Similarly, agents had to learn what paperwork was required for travel and entering certain restricted areas, and also to check that their own paperwork came up to scratch. They needed to know what kind of enemy presence there was in the area and, crucially, the attitude of the local police. Agents needed to keep their eyes open, talk to people, read the papers and generally get a sense of the environment.

It was particularly important to cultivate people who saw a real cross-section of life such as priests, innkeepers, barmaids, shopkeepers, medical staff such as doctors and nurses, railway workers and general grumblers and malcontents. Being aware of the rhythms of local life was vital, so agents would instantly notice if the normal routine had changed – if, for example, the postman was late, or someone had not put the cat out, or perhaps that there were strangers in the neighbourhood. This all might presage some enemy activity.

## Cover Stories in Action

Yvonne Cormeau, a wireless operator in the Gironde, usually used the cover of a district nurse, as it allowed her to move around quite freely. On one occasion, however, she took the role of a cowherd but had it pointed out to her by the farmer's wife that no woman who looked after cows would be able to afford a watch. The SOE trainers and her contact believed such details were crucial. However, she lost the job when she fell asleep, lost track of time and somehow managed to gain an extra cow through a hole in the fence, much to the annoyance of the neighbouring farmer.

Claude de Baissac, organizer of a network in Bordeaux, posed as a publicity agent, the vagueness of which seemed useful and perfectly acceptable to both the French and German police. However, his papers provided by London did not pass police examination. He was brought before the *commissaire de police,* who asked 'How long have you been here? You should tell London to be more careful' and promptly let him go. If all else failed, Captain Francis Cammaerts recommended feigning a case of tuberculosis, because the Germans seemed very frightened of the disease. Once, after getting off a train at Avignon station, when the control was taking rather a long time with his papers, he coughed and spluttered, bit his lip and then spat blood on the pavement. It looked rather impressive on the hard surface and his papers were rapidly returned and he was sent on his way.

## Disguise

It might occasionally be necessary to disguise an agent's appearance. If he was returning to work in his home town, quite drastic measures might be needed, such as plastic surgery. However, it was more likely that the disguise would be temporary, if it was known that the police had a description of the agent, or the agent was making contact with someone and did not want to be recognized. This, SOE believed, should only be done in an emergency. It also required some thought: indeed, much of the advice that applied to cover stories applied to the wearing of a

# Feigning Illness

**If the security forces were taking an unwanted interest in an agent's credentials, one way to discourage further investigation might be to feign illness. A hacking cough followed by spitting up blood might well convince the policeman that he was dealing with a case of tuberculosis and that discretion was the better part of valour.**

disguise, such as the need always to stay in character and wear clothing appropriate to the persona adopted.

For example, a workman should have rough, dirty hands and not be in white collar and tie. Stripes on a pinstripe suit could make an agent look taller, checked jackets could make them look broader. There were number of things that could be done quite quickly and simply to change the agent's appearance. Hair could be darkened with charcoal powder or lightened with peroxide. The same could be done to eyebrows. Make-up could be used on eyes, ears could be glued to the head, and noses could be flattened or widened by inserting nutshells with holes drilled in them into the nasal passage. Pads could be inserted into the checks to round out the face. Teeth could be stained

# Ruses and Alibis

The SOE trainers also advised that agents have a plausible alibi for whatever nefarious activity they were undertaking. It needed to be consistent with the agent's cover story and, of course, plausible. It was better if it was as near to the truth as possible. When Max Manus and Roy Nielsen of SOE's Norwegian Section attacked the German troopship *Donau* in Oslo Harbour on 15 January 1945, they gained access to the harbour by posing as electricians. This cover was given all the more legitimacy by the fact that they were accompanied by a genuine electrician, Kaare Halvorsen, who actually worked there.

To distract attention they used a number of ruses. The equipment – rubber boat, limpet mines, Sten Guns, grenades – was driven into the harbour by Alf Borgen in a trade van. Manus ensured that the van was followed by a car whose occupants caused a fuss and hooted ceaselessly. The irritated guards waved Borgen through in their hurry to deal with the car's driver and passenger, whose paperwork was, of course, impeccable. When Manus, Nielsen and Halvorsen entered the harbour, Nielsen engineered a spectacular slip on the ice. The guards roared with laughter, one helped him to his feet and no one checked his papers. The operation was a total success; the *Donau* was sunk and the saboteurs got away scot-free.

# Altering Your Appearance

**Fairly simple measures could achieve an effective change in an agent's appearance. Clothing could give a misleading impression – stripes to look taller, checks to look broader. Hair can be easily darkened with dye or even boot polish, or lightened with bleach.**

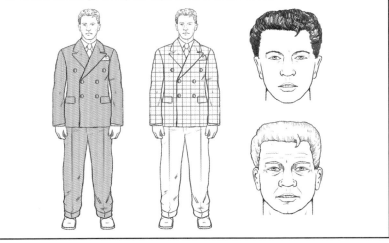

with iodine. SOE even produced a wrinkling cream that gave an aging effect by providing an unhealthy pallor. Lines could be drawn on with a make-up pencil. As an alternative, a more youthful appearance could be achieved with a close shave, the application of hot towels and alum and a dusting of talc. Moustaches and beards could change a face but took time to grow – indeed, SOE conducted a remarkably detailed study into beard growth. However, it was suggested that an agent might consider going into the field with a well-grown moustache and then simply shave it off.

### What to do if Being Followed

If agents suspected that they were being followed – and they were advised that they should always presume that they were – it was worth taking a number of precautions,

# Throwing a Tail

If the agent suspected that he was being tailed, he would then have to decide whether to abort the mission, or lose the tail. Certainly, he would not take a direct route to his destination. One possible means of losing a tail was to quickly board public transport or lose him in a crowd or large building such as a department store.

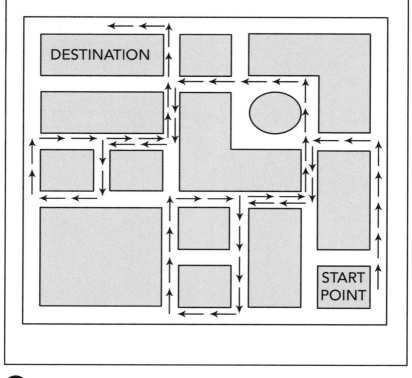

particularly when undertaking an operation. To check if they were being followed, agents could walk up an empty street, cross the road quickly or enter a café, restaurant or bar to check if anyone followed. Similarly, agents could enter a small shop and see if anyone hung around outside, particularly if they tried to conceal themselves. Another tactic was to leave something innocent behind in a shop, like a newspaper or stick, and return quickly for it. If agents reckoned that they were being followed, there were two courses of action available: attempt to lose the tail or accept the tail but cease all subversive activity immediately. In both cases it was essential not to let on that the tail had been spotted. Agents should not turn round hastily and should have an 'excuse' for stopping and checking, such as tying a shoelace, lighting a cigarette, even apparently checking out a pretty girl. If an agent decided to shake off a pursuer, there were a number of techniques: by running suddenly for public transport, boarding public transport naturally and smoothly, using the lifts in big stores with many exits, and moving quickly from open to crowded spaces.

### What to do if Stopped and Searched

It was possible an agent might be stopped and searched, either at a fixed checkpoint, in a random, snap

## Tactics Tip: Shaking Off a Tail

Fredrick Yeo-Thomas, an SOE agent in Paris, shook off his tail on at least four occasions. On the first, he and fellow agent Georges Pichard noticed a man fall in behind them about 20 yards back. They made a few detours to ensure that they were really being followed and once sure that he was interested, decided to lose him. They made their way to the Madeleine Metro station. Pichard dived into the metro and Yeo-Thomas quickly crossed the road, forcing the tail to decide who to follow. He chose Yeo-Thomas, who, with an hour to kill, decided to take his pursuer for a long, fast walk. After he had sweated his tail (the man was wearing a heavy grey overcoat), he decided to lose him. So he dashed in the Printemps department store and made his way into the basement while the tail struggled through a group of shoppers. Yeo-Thomas slipped through one of the service passages reserved for employees and made his escape.

# Concealed Items

**SOE and OSS devised numerous ways of concealing messages and disguising equipment. OSS produced a knife that could be worn comfortably inside a shoe's insole, sandwiched between two pieces of leather.**

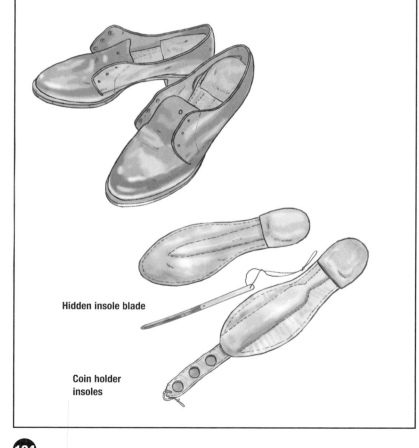

Hidden insole blade

Coin holder insoles

search or because of specific enemy suspicions. Of course, it was better not to be carrying anything suspicious, but if it was unavoidable, there were two possible approaches: either attempt to dispose of the incriminating material or hide it as effectively as possible. In the first case, the article must be accessible, either held in the hand or a pocket, and ready to dropped or palmed off onto an innocent passer-by. It was worthwhile holding a message on something edible so that it could easily be disposed of. Bulky items like radios in suitcases could at least be abandoned. If the material was well hidden it should pass a routine search in the street. Care needed to be taken when sewing messages into the seams of clothing, however. SOE produced a whole range of products such as pens, pipes, tools, suitcases, toiletries and the like, which had compartments that could conceal messages and small items. They even designed special bundles of faggots, gramophones and vacuum cleaners to conceal radios.

The agent was to find out what the purpose of the search was and act accordingly. The reaction should be consistent with the agent's cover, feigning annoyance, indignation, indifference or whatever. Clearly, the reactions of those being searched were being observed, so it was vital not to show nervousness or relief once the search had finished. It might

be possible to confuse the searchers by dropping an article into a pile of already-searched items. It might also be to the agent's advantage to be found in possession of some minor incriminating item such as liquor or currency, thereby distracting attention from anything more damning.

## Establishing a Network

Once established in the local community, the agent might be preparing for some kind of operation requiring observation and planning. More likely, they would be setting about the business of establishing a local network. This required the recruitment of agents.

### Recruitment of Agents

As the success of the network was dependent on the quality of its members, SOE urged its agents to take their time in selecting those to approach. It was important to work out what might motivate a prospective agent and engage them accordingly. Indeed, it might even be advantageous to have them suggest what help they could offer. The key motivators were considered to be: patriotism, political or religious beliefs, hatred of the Germans and a desire for adventure – particularly amongst the young.

Material needs might well be the dominant motive, given the severe privations suffered in occupied Europe. So, regular financial support might be very useful to some, particularly when coupled with the other, perhaps purer, motives. It might not necessarily be money but goods such as food, tobacco, petrol or medicine. SOE made a distinction between payments that might be necessary so that the recruit could afford to play a full part in operations, and baser motives such as greed.

Bribery might be necessary on occasion, although a man who had been bribed could never be deemed entirely trustworthy. Other, baser instincts, such as the procurement of sexual favours or fear, could be used – but always the services of someone outside the organization, in order to avoid any dangerous consequences. Although threats or blackmail could be useful, too, these methods did not make for a reliable helper.

Arthur Stagg, a wireless operator working in the 'Wireless' circuit in Lille, played on a number of these motivations, such as greed, patriotism and fear, when cornered. When his radio transmitter was discovered by French plainclothes police while he was travelling by train, he tried to persuade them that it was sound equipment for cinema films. When this did not work offered them 1000 francs apiece and appealed to their patriotism. This worked but he backed it up by flashing the butt

of his revolver at them. They allowed him to get off the train at the next station without incident.

## The Approach
Having divined the motivation of possible recruits, it was time for the agent to approach them. The process was dangerous. The agent should build his network slowly, taking particular care in the early stages. He should retain the initiative and be wary of anyone who approached him, a favourite tactic of *agent provocateurs*.

**Suitability** The man recruited should be appropriate for the job, not shoehorned into an unsuitable role. Nor should a newly recruited person be kept hanging around with nothing to do. The agent needed to collect information and get a sense of what motivated the person they hoped to recruit.

SOE deemed it particularly important to be aware of the attachments of any woman recruited, and warned of recruiting one motivated purely by sentiment. It was also advised to avoid anyone who was even suspected of working for another Resistance organization.

**Carefulness** The actual approach was tricky and needed to done in such a way that the recruiter did not commit and could back out at any time. If possible, the concrete suggestions should come from the recruit. The recruiter should never overpersuade; in fact, it was better to be honest about the dangers. Nor should he give away information about the organization and should initially use a cut-out address (see p130).

**Reliability** The instructors suggested that the agent needed to use careful judgement as to whether an initiation or oath-swearing ceremony should be used. Early tasks given to the new recruit should be simple and harmless, both to test his reliability and make him feel that he was useful to the organization.

## Discipline

It was also necessary to maintain discipline. Agents needed to be aware of the power of the organization both to protect them and, if necessary, punish those who betrayed it. Success should be praised but not overly so. Honest failure should be accepted and the organizer should commiserate with the agent. If failure was down to nerves or stress, the agent should be rested and continue to be paid. If the task was beyond their capabilities or intelligence, they should be given an easier job or simply told to lie low because the enemy was after him.

Agents discovered to be traitors could be bought off or frightened, although these courses of action were deemed risky. The most straightforward solution was to kill them. However, SOE advised that it was better not to let things get to this stage and to stress instead the long arm of the organization and its capacity for vengeance early on.

Roger Landes, an SOE agent, knew that the former head of the 'Scientist' network, André Grandclément, had been working for the Germans since September 1943. The Resistance finally caught up with the man who had betrayed so many in August 1944. After a long interrogation, in which Grandclément admitted working for the Germans, Landes' group decided the traitor should be shot. The *Maquis* did not have any problem with executing Grandclément and his bodyguard, but balked at shooting his wife. There was no question of letting her go, so Landes had to kill her himself, using his pistol for the first and only time in the war. He did not sleep for a week afterwards.

# The Organization in Action

Once the agent started to establish a network, he would have to work out what type of activity to undertake in line with general SOE and Allied policy. It was also heavily dependent on local conditions, particularly the nature of the terrain and the enemy presence in the area. In terms of the organization outlined below, SOE was thinking in terms of a fairly large regional set-up.

# Making Payment

SOE had no problem with the idea of paying new agents. Indeed, while recognizing patriotism was the best motive, it was felt that providing monetary support did no harm at all. The new recruit might well need the financial support and it also provided an extra measure of control. It was recommended to pay a regular salary rather than make irregular payments for services rendered. This might lead to claims being made that would have to be investigated, although SOE did not rule out the payment of bonuses. SOE saw the relationship as comparable to that between a good employer and employee, believing that the leader should offer support in time of illness and to look after the recruit's dependents in case of arrest, including the possibility of organizing escapes.

Payment should be made punctually and if, for any reason, the flow of cash was interrupted, the recruit should be given a frank explanation. Cash in person was the best method of payment and the recipient should be warned of the dangers of spending too freely and obviously. It was advised never to let one agent know what another was being paid.

The newly recruited agent would require some training in security measures and enemy counter-espionage techniques. If required to undertake a mission, such as sabotage, specific training would be required. Training in combat skills was difficult to organize in urban areas, although it might be undertaken relatively freely in the wild. However, most adult European males had had military training and it was possible to gain a reasonable familiarity with a weapon like the Sten Gun without actually firing it on a range.

### Operations and Support

An organization basically divided into operational and support sections. In terms of operations, there might be a propaganda section, a minor sabotage and passive resistance section, a major operations section and, perhaps a paramilitary unit. In terms of support sections, there would need to be an internal communications section made up of couriers – people running possible 'letter-boxes' such as cafes or kiosks and accommodation addresses to receive mail. There would be a security section to keep an eye on the enemy and guard against infiltration. Depending on the location, there might be a reception team, responsible for organizing and meeting the dropping or landing of agents or supplies.

The organization would require some sort of quartermaster section, holding and hiding stores and distributing equipment as needed. Closely related to this would be the transport section. Petrol might well have to be hoarded for operations and emergencies. For a large organization, a finance section would be necessary to manage the money and the payment of agents. Indeed, as the organization grew, specific talent spotters might be employed in a recruiting section.

A medical section would also be necessary, particularly if the group was undertaking any paramilitary activity. Additionally, a special section with specific responsibility for emergencies, for organizing safe-houses, escape routes and the like would be needed. Depending on the circumstances, these sections might consist of large numbers of agents or only one or two.

Security, as ever, was a key SOE concern. All members needed to have a knowledge of self-defence and the organization's security procedures. However, they should avoid carrying arms unless in a situation were no cover story was available. The carrying of guns seems to have been very much a matter of personal choice when working undercover. The situation was obviously different if the agent was operating with the Maquis after D-Day or with Partisans in the Balkans. Henri Diacono, a wireless operator in Paris, never carried a gun and felt very much vindicated when he was stopped and searched coming out of the Metro. He noted that 'if I had had a gun I would have been lost'.

## Maintaining Security

The agents must not attempt to learn more about the organization than strictly necessary. They should always use the correct cover names and never contact members of other organizations without permission. The agents needed to be vigilant and report any suspicious incidents. If the balloon went up, they had to know what to do, what warning signals were involved, who needed to be warned, where to go (to safe-houses, what cover stories to use), what contacts and activities to drop and finally how to re-establish contacts. The leader had a number of additional responsibilities – indeed it would be his plan the agents would carry out in an emergency. He would decide how the situation affected contacts and plans, and which of these should be dropped or postponed. He would also warn contacts to take prearranged emergency action. He would clear up incriminating evidence, destroying materials and the like. He was responsible for finding out why an agent had been captured and if he had talked. If possible, he would organize a rescue attempt.

## Cooperation with Resistance Organizations

Cooperation was not always guaranteed. SOE and the Norwegian Resistance movement, *Milorg (Militær organisasjon)* – The Military Organization) disagreed over long-term policy. SOE, particularly in the early years, was keen to be aggressive and tie down large German forces. However, following early failures and penetration by the security forces, the leadership of *Milorg* came to believe that there was a need to rebuild and reinforce. The intention was to build up an organization, an army-in-being, that could support an Allied invasion. In the meantime *Milorg* would train, arm and prepare for that day, eschewing an active policy of sabotage in the meantime. This was not wholly acceptable to SOE or even elements

of the Norwegian Government-in-Exile, who felt Norway needed to make a more active contribution to the Allied cause.

These contradictory positions were reconciled to an extent by the formation of the Anglo-Norwegian Collaboration Committee, which enabled SOE to undertake a programme of raiding and sabotage with a degree of local support, while members of the Norwegian Section provided training for the resistance. When it became clear Norway would not be liberated by Allied invasion, *Milorg* stepped up its activities in order to keep large numbers of Germans away from the campaign in Northwest Europe.

## Security

At the core of the organization would be the head of the network's most trusted 'staff officers', who would run one or more of the sections. These should be limited to about four to six men. Most organizations would be fairly small or mission-specific. The difficulty was in getting the balance right between security and efficiency. Efficient operations relied on close contact, whereas security was improved by watertight compartmentalization. It was, overall, probably better to err on the side of security. The organizer should endeavour to keep the organization as small as possible, and he should only ever deal with his trusted staff officers. They should be able to recruit independently, with the details, although not the names, of new agents, approved at the top.

The organizer should set the limits of contact between the sections. Individual agents should have the minimum number contacts and

# Concealed Weapons

**SOE also produced a host of small concealed bladed weapons, such as the lapel and thumb knives. These could be used to slash or stab suddenly at an enemy, particularly at his face. They could, of course, also be used against vehicle tyres.**

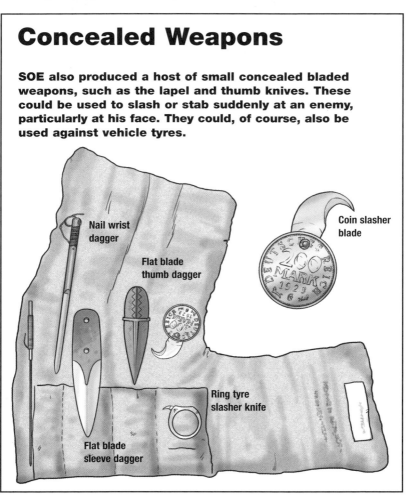

Nail wrist dagger

Flat blade thumb dagger

Coin slasher blade

Ring tyre slasher knife

Flat blade sleeve dagger

know as little as possible about the organization as a whole. The maximum use of cut-outs was recommended. The SOE definition of a cut-out ran thus:

> *A cut-out, or intermediary, forms the link between two agents or between an agent and the outside world. He may know very little about the organization and just carry messages, or he may be a liaison officer who is able to answer questions and take decisions; but the important thing is that he undertake no other subversive activity.*

The reasons for employing cut-outs was to separate agents from each other and to put a barrier between the authorities and the agent. The cut-out should be someone who could easily liaise between the two, such as a waiter or taxi-driver, or a professional who might be consulted by anyone, whatever their background, such as a priest, lawyer, doctor or bank manager.

## Procedures for Meetings

Agents, however, would inevitably have to meet in person now and again. More information could be passed, the correct emphasis could be placed on material and the whole process was immediate. Also, face-to-face contact was on occasion a psychological necessity. However, meetings were fraught with danger:

face-to-face contact might allow the enemy to identify a hitherto unknown contact and there was the possibility that the meeting might be a trap. SOE did not recommend meeting in very public places such as railway stations, hotels, post-offices and, in particularl, that location so disliked by SOE, the brothel. Small cafes or bars were better. Better still were the street, gardens, parks, churches, swimming-baths, museums, the beach or a private house or office hired by a third party.

However, the agent should always have plausible reasons for being at any location chosen for a meeting. Prior to the meeting, security measures should be taken, and the rendezvous (RV) location should be checked beforehand. Anti-surveillance tactics should be used and agents should always be aware of the possibility of the use of concealed microphones. It was recommended to turn on a gramophone or run the bath when indoors.

As an additional precaution, the time and date should be arranged by separate measures. SOE recommended an old communist trick that involved adding an hour to the time of the meeting, so that the police would turn up an hour late. It was also necessary to be punctual and limit the time that the agent had to wait and be exposed to danger.

# Concealing Messages

**Everyday items can be used to conceal messages. Tubes of toothpaste, collar studs and door keys are unlikely to arouse any obvious suspicion and should pass all but the most detailed examination of an agent's possessions.**

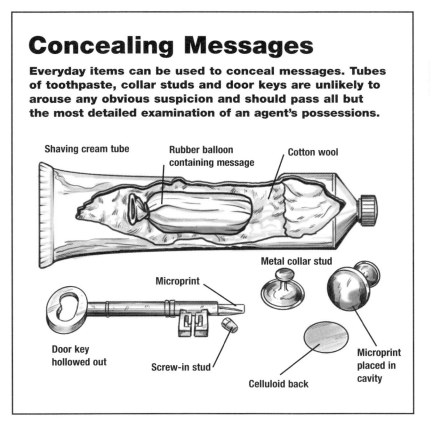

Shaving cream tube

Rubber balloon containing message

Cotton wool

Metal collar stud

Microprint

Door key hollowed out

Screw-in stud

Celluloid back

Microprint placed in cavity

The agents should have a system of warnings, for example, not wearing gloves might mean danger. The RV should be changed frequently and there should be an alternate meeting point in case of any accidents. The agents, if acquainted, should quickly establish a cover conversation. It was important not to whisper and to smile and laugh as much as possible. The passing of messages should be done discreetly, in the toilet possibly or by the exchange of identical briefcases, matchboxes or newspapers. The issue was a little more complicated for agents who did not know one another. Accurate descriptions of each other were required.

A short, simple and incongruous password should be used – and as naturally as possible. Again security precautions should be taken. If the agent had any suspicions at all, he should abandon the RV.

A colleague might check out the location beforehand or the agent might have himself followed to check whether he had picked up a tail. He should not accept the outsider's recommendation of time and place. It might be wise to send a cut-out to bring the contact to an alternative meeting place or possibly intercept him en route and take him elsewhere.

### The Cell Structure

SOE also recommended that the organization protect itself by adopting a cell structure. This both aided security and allowed for a degree of expansion, if required. One man inside a cell could recruit another outsider, who would then recruit his own cell. The only contact would be between those two and thus it was hoped the security forces would struggle to trace the rest of the organization if one member came under suspicion. In times of rapid expansion, for example if liberation was near, a method

# Passing Messages – Switching Briefcases

**One method of exchanging messages is to switch identical items, as in the well-known briefcase swap. The agents stop next to one other and simply exchange briefcases, without acknowledging one another before departing. It is simple, quick and, when it is done properly, goes entirely unnoticed.**

of 'radiation' could begin, whereby the cell members would recruit more than one new cell. This was commensurately more dangerous, but allowed for a large increase in numbers if one was attempting to build a secret army.

Cells needed to be small, only three to eight individuals. The members would carry out their task and also collect information that would be passed back to the leader. They needed to be aware of their own security and report any sign of a threat, such as a colleague not turning up for work, as soon as possible. The original recruiter would be the contact and his only contact should be his original recruit. Given the chain-like nature of the series of cells, some cells might be isolated if there was a break. Some sort of general response would be needed in such an eventuality; SOE suggested an emergency address that might be advertised in a certain place in a particular newspaper.

The cell system was slow and cumbersome but it provided a good deal of security and was suitable for a relatively simple campaign of low-level sabotage and propaganda.

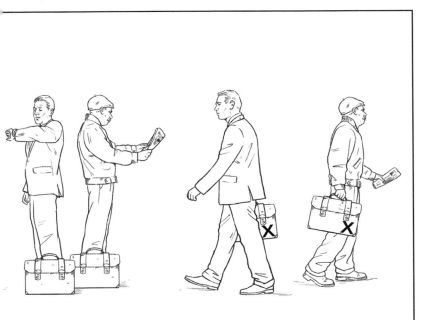

# Gestapo Set-Up

The very real dangers of meeting an unknown contact were well illustrated in Oslo on 17 November 1944.

Two Norwegian SOE agents, Gregers Gram and Edvard Tallaksen, met with two German communist deserters at the Plass Café in the Grünnaløka area of Oslo. The whole thing, however, was a set-up by the Gestapo, who wanted to establish that the two agents' bona fides had been faked.

As the Gestapo moved in, a gun battle ensued. Although the agents killed two of their German pursuers, Gram was shot through the throat and died, while Tallaksen was wounded and taken prisoner. He later committed suicide by strangling himself with his own shirt.

It also provided a preparatory structure for armed revolt. When the Allied invasion approached, the organization needed to be able to switch quickly from subversive work to supporting the attack. Under these circumstances, the normal rather slow method of communication between cells would have be replaced by something more immediate. Cut-outs would probably be eliminated and key men put in touch with one another. A plan of key points to be seized should be prepared, and ample supplies of weapons, ammunition and explosives made available.

## Communications

Once an organization had been set up, it was vital that communications were established with the United Kingdom. This allowed instructions to be given, information passed both ways and agent or equipment drops arranged. Although this could be achieved by courier, the principal and quickest method was by wireless telegraphy (WT). The WT operator was an important and highly trained asset, and special precautions needed to be put in place to protect him or her. SOE recommended that WT operators not be used for other work, although this was often very much more honoured in the breach than in the observance.

### WT Procedures

Messages had to be short – 150 to 400 letters – and transmitted in less than five minutes. The operators were on a strict timetable to avoid the home receiver stations being

# Resistance Cells

**To prevent the rolling-up off the whole organization,
should one agent be captured, it was safer to operate
in small cells. Most agents would know only very few
of their most immediate colleagues. Only the cell's
leader would have contact with other agents.**

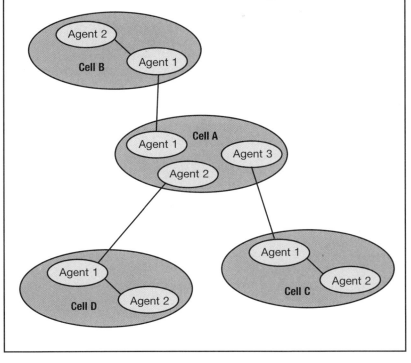

swamped. The set itself was usually
disguised as a suitcase although, as
mentioned above, SOE came up with
a number of ingenious methods of

disguise. It was suggested that the
set was buried on arrival, although
this made its regular use a bit
awkward. The aerial should be

**137**

# Equipment Profile:
# The Mark II (B2)
# Suitcase Transceiver

The Mark II was probably the pinnacle of clandestine WT sets. It was introduced in 1942 and served until the end of the war. It was simple to use, capable of long-distance communication and effectively screened out German interference. It was usually camouflaged in a small suitcase divided into four compartments. The left compartment housed the 18m (60ft) aerial wire, the key, headset and the various leads and wires required. The two middle compartments held the transmitter on the top and the receiver at the bottom. On the right were the batteries.

### Standard Features
**Coverage:** 3–15.5 megacycles in three wave bands for the receiver and 3–16 megacycles for the transmitter.
**Power output:** 30 watts max.
**Power supply:** 97–250 volts.
**Weight:** 14.5kg (32lbs).
**Dimensions:**
**Transmitter:** 23cm x 18cm x 13cm (9in x 7in x 5in).
**Receiver:** 23cm x 11cm x 13cm (9in x 4.5in x 5in).
**Battery:** 25cm x 10cm x 13cm (10in x 4in x 5in).

camouflaged and SOE again came up with number of disguises such as a clothesline. The radio operator's cover job had to explain his irregular hours, and SOE recommended that he live with friends, as the tapping of the Morse key was distinctly audible.

The operator should also move himself and his set regularly. It was also worthwhile to have a number of sets hidden in a number of locations as the radios were heavy and conspicuous. The sets were usually about 18kg (40lbs) in weight,

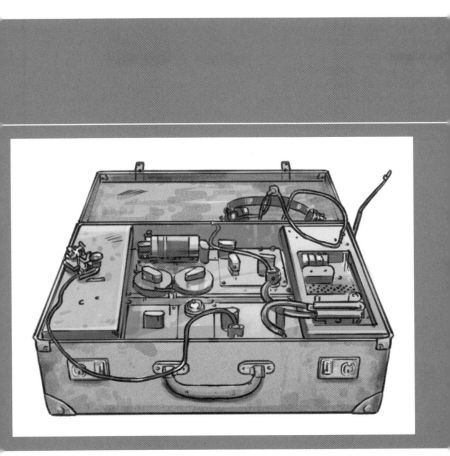

with dimensions 61cm x 30cm x 15cm (2ft x 1ft by 6in), and were powered either directly from the mains or by battery. The use of the mains had its disadvantages, however. One trick the Germans used when trying to locate a radio operator was to cut the power to different parts of the town and if the radio operator's transmission stopped suddenly, they knew that he was in comparatively small area of the town. So, operators mainly preferred to use batteries.

These could be recharged as one might a car battery, or by petrol or steam generators. SOE did also produce hand and pedal generators.

As mentioned above, the operator worked to a strict timetable and needed to keep the messages short and without superfluous words. The transmissions were, of course, in code but the quality of those codes was quite poor in the early years. Leo Marks, SOE's code expert, was horrified that agents used a simple letter/number substitution system based on a poem memorized by the agent. These were relatively straightforward to break and once the Germans had worked out the key, the messages could be decoded at will. Leo Marks' solution was the invention of the 'One-time Pad', which was a piece of silk with a series of transpositions codes that were married to a copy held at Home Station, which would be used only once and then destroyed. Even if captured, the agent would be unlikely to remember the codes that had been used previously.

### Enemy Radio Detection Systems

Enemy counter-measures relied on a number of techniques, some quite sophisticated, and others less so. These included: a ban on all private transmitters; checkpoints to catch W/T sets in transit; the recording of messages and attempts to decipher the codes; and the above-mentioned

# Pedal Generator for Radio

**In rural areas or to avoid dependence on the mains, SOE radio operators would need to charge their radio batteries. Steam and petrol-driven generators were produced, but for pure simplicity the pedal-driven version had a great deal to recommend it.**

method of switching off the power in a suspected locality. Probably the most serious threat was direction-finding (DF). Fixed DF stations would attempt to triangulate the approximate area from which the agent was transmitting, and then mobile teams, using vehicle-mounted or even hand-held equipment, would close in on the transmitter. The agent would thus have constantly to keep on the move, and when he did transmit, it was worth having some security around him. Colleagues should look out for approaching

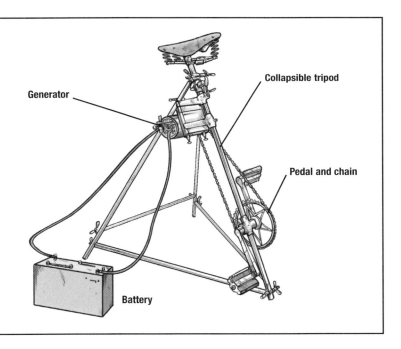

Generator

Collapsible tripod

Pedal and chain

Battery

DF teams and be ready to help him escape or move the set. It was pointed out that the operator was considerably more important than his equipment. Suspicious material should be kept separate from the set and the operator should have a pistol to hand.

Jean Holley, a radio operator, was picked up by a DF team in Lyon. He was told by the Germans that their main listening centre in Berlin had identified the direction he was transmitting from and once they had narrowed down the location, a DF van was sent out to find him.

He and his team were followed and Holley was arrested at the railway station at Annecy. As he tried to escape, he was tackled by a large German who punched him in the face and said, 'You bastard, I've been after you for four months.' The Germans showed him a whole cabinet full of his transmissions that they had not been able to decode. Holley was tortured and later handed over to the Italians, which probably explains his survival.

The circuit's organizer needed to protect his WT operator, although he

# Concealing a Radio

An agent needed to develop a local identity that would allow him or her to function as part of the local populace while carrying out his or her work as a a an agent. Faggots of firewood, for example, could be used to conceal a wireless set when the radio needed to be moved from one location to another. Care had be taken to ensure that the faggots corresponded to the type found in the local district.

# Mission Profile:
# The *Englandspiel*

The dangers of a radioman being turned are well illustrated by the *Englandspiel* counter-espionage operation undertaken by the *Abwehr* (German military intelligence) in the Netherlands. Huub Lauwers was picked up by the Germans and 'agreed' to continue to operate his set, confident that London would notice when he left out his security check. London did not, as at this stage the Secret Intelligence Service was handling SOE's communications. Agents were dropped into the Netherlands and continued to be captured by the Germans, and many more were turned. London even failed to notice when Lauwers transmitted the group 'CAUGHT' on three occasions. In all, 52 agents were captured and SOE achieved virtually nothing between March 1942 and May 1943. Two agents even managed to escape back to Britain only to find themselves in Brixton Prison until D-Day was launched, as the Germans sent a message saying they had gone over to the Gestapo. It was SOE's most incompetent episode of the war.

would expect his radio man to be a capable individual who could look after himself.

Radio men should communicate directly as little as possible. Instead, they should use cut-outs and dead-letter boxes. The organizer might have to find spare parts for the radio or even arrange for its repair or replacement. The organizer and operator should come to an arrangement as to who was responsible for encoding and decoding. The operator should also ensure that escape routes were available in case of an emergency.

The operator should have as little to do with the rest of the organization as possible and recruit his own cell to help with look-outs, protection and transport of the radio sets.

If captured, the radio operator might very well not be immediately executed, as expected. Instead, he would often be 'persuaded' to work for the Germans and 'played back' against SOE. For this reason, the radio operator had a number of security checks that could be omitted to warn Home Station, should he fall into enemy hands.

**O**n many missions the operatives' objective was intelligence gathering – obtaining useful information about the enemy, such as: its forces' strengths, locations and movements; the location, capacity and methods of its industry; the location, capacity and operation of its transport; the morale, beliefs and motivation of its personnel; and the numbers, locations, capabilities and tactical use of its weaponry.

Operatives conducted three main intelligence-gathering missions: general intelligence, non-operative mission-specific and operative mission-specific. In the first, mission operatives obtained information that generally benefited their host nation's war effort, for example, by collecting data on enemy morale.

In the second, mission operatives acquired specific information that would facilitate the successful undertaking of a particular mission to be carried out by regular forces; for example, operatives landed by midget submarine on the Normandy coast to take beach samples that would facilitate the planned Allied D-Day landings. In the third, mission operatives gathered specific

..................................

**Intelligence gathering was one of the chief tasks of an undercover operative. Specialist techniques and equipment were needed for agents to function effectively.**

# 4

**Obtaining information about the enemy and their plans is one of the key functions of the secret agent and Resistance fighter.**

**Intelligence Gathering**

# British Intelligence Services

**During World War II, SOE was not the only British agency that employed secret operatives on intelligence-gathering missions behind enemy lines; the Secret Intelligence Services (MI5 and MI6) also carried out such activities.**

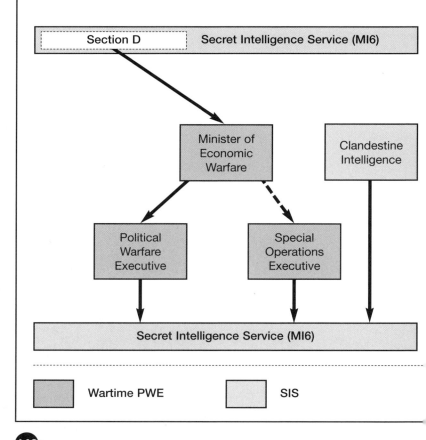

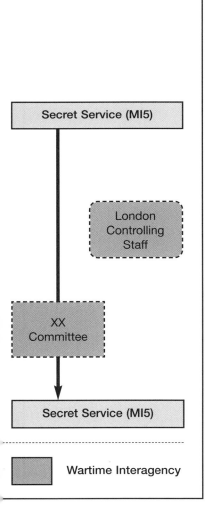

Secret Service (MI5)

London Controlling Staff

XX Committee

Secret Service (MI5)

Wartime Interagency

information that would facilitate the successful undertaking of a particular operative mission, such as a raid.

### General Intelligence
Operatives gathered an enormous amount of general intelligence about the enemy, principally through visual observation. This involved operatives getting close enough to the target to make a lengthy visual observation without being detected. Operative visual observation intelligence-gathering encompassed two principal methods – long-range and close-range surveillance. In the former, agents observed the target from a distance (typically several miles), using binoculars or telescopes, whereas in the latter the operative got sufficiently close to visually observe the target with the naked eye. The former method was less risky for the operative but the amount of precise data that could be obtained was more restricted than with the latter. The mode selected depended much on the circumstances, such as the type of intelligence desired, the agents' capabilities and the terrain.

## Long-range Surveillance
Irrespective of whether the mission involved long- or close-range surveillance, the operative first had to approach the target without being detected, employing the skills and techniques discussed in the previous

# Spider Hole OP

A Spider Hole was a one-man observation post (OP). It consisted of a standard-sized foxhole that was, apart from a small vision port or slit, completely covered by wood or plastic sheeting, on top of which was placed camouflaging foliage.

Observation port

two chapters. If the mission was to undertake protracted long-range visual surveillance (lasting days or even weeks), operatives would construct a camouflaged and concealed hide or observation post (OP) located in an overwatch position. Working at night, the operatives would dig a covered dugout that had a small viewing spacing facing the target; a large bush or tree might also help to conceal the hide. Operatives could construct various types of OP, such as the Spider-Hole, Tent-Type and Bunker-Type, depending on the size of the team, length of observation, equipment carried, time available, soil/vegetation type and terrain conditions. In areas of likely enemy surveillance, operatives might, in addition to their efforts to camouflage their OP, also camouflage their skin to prevent any colour contrast being evident to a skilled enemy observer (see *Tactics Tip: Individual Skin Camouflage*, p151).

Irrespective of the OP type, the operatives had to conceal any signs of its construction, for example disposing of the removed soil in an inconspicuous fashion away from the

# Tent-Type OP

**The Tent-Type observation post is made for more than one observer. Branches can be used to create the frame and a parachute used for making the inner lining. A slight arch in the cover increases the available space on the inside of the position. The outside should be covered in local materials so that the post blends into the surroundings.**

Telescope

Camouflage

# Bunker-Type OP

**A Bunker-type OP was a sophisticated position that required extensive construction time and material to complete. It consisted of a large excavated space, enough to house several men, lined with sandbags or plastic sheeting to strengthen the structure and to keep out water; it was covered with a substantial wooded roof covered with earth and foliage that included at least one viewing port or slit.**

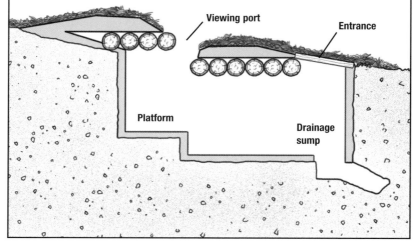

OP. They would also have to conceal any boot-prints and reloosen tramped-down ground. This could be labour-intensive, with operatives perhaps even straightening every blade of grass that had been tramped down. During late 1943, for example, Allied motor launches based in Corsica inserted an eight-man OSS team onto the German-held island of Elba, off the western coast of Italy. Trekking up to the summit of Mount Capanne in western Elba, the team established an OP that looked out northeast to the harbour of Portoferraio; here they radioed back information regarding any shipping movement to OSS HQ in Corsica by quick pre-arranged letter-

# Tactics Tip:
# Individual Skin Camouflage

Operatives established in an OP for a visual observation mission often needed to camouflage their skin to prevent them being detected by a skilled enemy observer. The agents would use two differently coloured cam-sticks that mirrored the local foliage and apply them to all exposed skin areas with a striping or splotching technique (or a combination of the two).

Operatives were trained to lighten shadowy areas of their faces (around the eyes, and under the chin and nose) and darken shiny areas (chin, nose, cheeks and forehead). If standard cam-sticks were not available, operatives would improvise with charcoal or burnt cork, chewed leaves and grass, or mud.

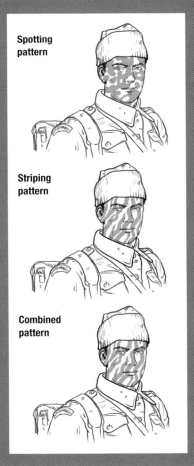

Spotting
pattern

Striping
pattern

Combined
pattern

# Observation Devices

**SOE secret operatives employed various personal observation devices, including binoculars, monoculars and periscopes. Seen here on the left is the British Taylor-Hobson 6x30 No.2 Mk.II 1941 binoculars, and on the right the OSS Wollenstock Hester monocular with its carrying case.**

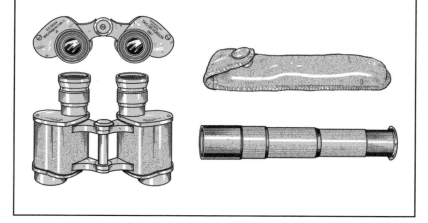

coded radio messages. Several clandestine maritime resupply missions kept the OP functioning for six weeks before the Germans discovered the hide, forcing the team to escape and be extracted by sea.

## Equipment

Operatives established in an OP for protracted long-range surveillance could employ a range of devices to observe the target, including binoculars (such as the 6x30 No.2 Mk.II), a monocular (like the British Infra-Red Tabby Mark K), a telescope (such as the OSS Wollenstock Hester), or a periscope. Long-range intelligence gathering worked in situations where the agents did not have to obtain really detailed

# Monocular

SOE's Tabby Mark K was a hand-held infrared monocular that was carried in a sturdy leather case. Its high-voltage integral power unit was driven by three specially designed batteries named Zamboni piles.

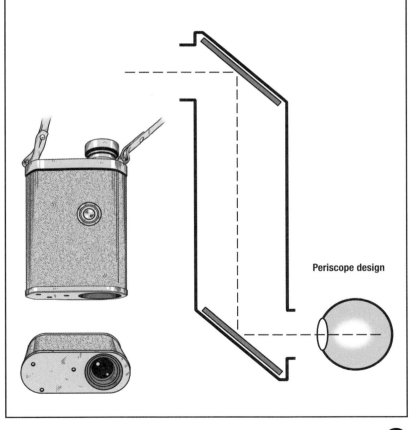

Periscope design

# Tactical Sketch

**One valuable product delivered from secret operative visual observations of an enemy target was the creation of accurate 2-D sketches that depicted the enemy's tactical situation, including the terrain (particularly dead ground), the location of key enemy weapons (together with their arcs of fire), and the positioning of obstacles such as wire.**

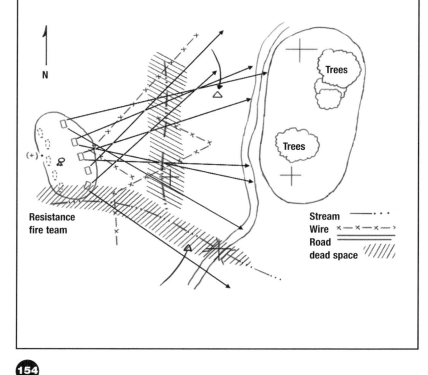

N

Trees

Trees

Resistance
fire team

Stream ——— · ·
Wire ×—×—×—›
Road ═══
dead space ⁄⁄⁄⁄⁄

or small-scale visual information; the Allies often used it to observe aircraft arriving or departing an airfield, or shipping arrivingat or departing a port. With the most powerful telescopes, operatives could observe targets up to 32km (20 miles) away. On 8 December 1943, for example, eight OSS operatives landed on Gorgona island, 32km (20 miles) offshore from Livorno on the northwestern Italian coast, and established an OP. Using a high-powered telescope, they observed German shipping entering/leaving the port and sent coded reports by radio back to the OSS base in northern Corsica.

### Information Obtained

This type of operative intelligence-gathering mission delivered a range of useful products. If observing an enemy airfield or harbour, operatives produced time-sensitive 'immediate' tactical intelligence that needed to be communicated quickly by coded radio messages. It took a German aircraft based in Italy, for example, just five minutes to reach Allied-held Corsica, so the OSS OPs on the island of Elba needed to communicate a take-off immediately. With other missions, the intelligence acquired was less time-sensitive. In these missions, operatives produced detailed 2-D and 3-D sketches of the target, as well as annotating pre-printed terrain maps with enemy

positions to produce a 'defence overlay'. These would depict all enemy positions, including their principal weapons' killing zones and arcs of fire, personnel locations, obstacles (like wire, walls and ditches), command centres and OPs, as well as key terrain features, such as concealed approaches, withdrawal and reinforcement routes, dead ground, and natural obstacles (such as rivers, canals, ditches and embankments). To augment these sketches and overlays, operatives might also take photographs of the target using special small cameras such as the Minox Riga sub-miniature spy camera.

## Close-range Surveillance

Operatives undertaking a close-range visual observation of the target would not go to the trouble of constructing a hide; they would only be observing the target for a short time (from a few days down to just a few minutes) and they would be so close that any hide was likely to be detected. At best, they would construct a scrape-OP or simply hide behind natural features or vegetation. Even in the latter case, however, operative observers would still employ traditional military concealment and cover exploitation techniques. Operative close-range visual target observation came in two forms; covert and disguised. In the former, the agent would approach the target using secrecy and

# Scrape-OP

**A scrape-OP utilized the enlargement of a natural depression in the ground to allow one prone soldier to occupy this position covertly. Over the top of this depression, the occupier fixed canvas or plastic sheeting tied down by pegs and lateral ropes; finally, camouflage netting, top soil and foliage were added to disguise the position. The main benefit of this type of OP is that troops can construct it quickly and easily.**

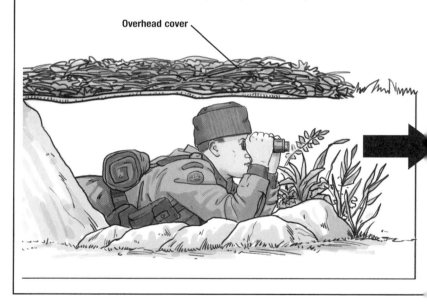

Overhead cover

concealment, typically at night, and then as first light approached select a suitable location for one or more one-man scrape-OPs; once the surveillance had been accomplished, the operatives would remove any traces of their presence, and steal away at night.

## Support from the Resistance

In contrast, during disguised close-range visual target observation, the

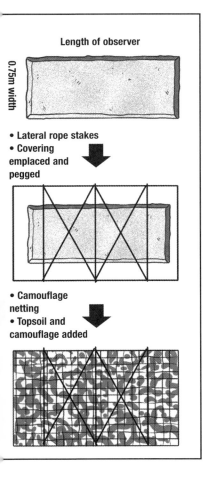

**Length of observer**

0.75m width

• Lateral rope stakes
• Covering emplaced and pegged

• Camouflage netting
• Topsoil and camouflage added

operatives openly approached the target, relying on their disguise as enemy personnel or a local civilian to avoid, or limit, enemy attention. Experience showed that one key component to success in this

type of mission was the use of inconspicuous personnel who employed a convincing cover story. This approach worked for Margarethe Kelder, a member of the Partisan Action Netherlands (PAN) Resistance group. In addition to smuggling downed Allied airmen into northern Belgium, PAN's female members acted as couriers and intelligence-gatherers. In early September 1944, as described in *Tactics Tip: Successful Overt Close-range Visual Target Observation* (see p159), PAN tasked Kelder and another female Resistance member to confirm the presence of a German anti-aircraft battery in woods near Eindhoven.

Instead of direct long- or close-range surveillance, operatives could also obtain general information by exploiting the intelligence-gathering capabilities of Resistance groups. Many operative missions – such as the 1944–45 'Jedburgh' and 'Sussex' teams described in *Tactics Tip: Intelligence-Gathering* (p160) and *Mission Profile: The Top Intelligence-Gatherers* (p161) – established agents among such groups to support their activities. On 23 March 1945, the OSS two-man team 'Doctor' parachuted into the Kitzbühl region of Austria, where they linked up with Austrians developing an embryonic guerrilla network; the two supply drops they requested from London brought weapons and munitions, as well as binoculars with which to

# Correct Use of Cover

In their pre-deployment training, special operatives received training in the most effective ways of employing various types of natural cover to facilitate an intelligence-gathering mission.

A. Observing from behind tree.
B. From a ditch observing over broken edge with background.
C. Observing over a crest at a point where it is broken or grassy.
D. Observing prone under the crossbar of fence.
E. Keeping weapon below line of site.
F. Observing through bushes.
G. Observing around right side of rock.

A

B

C

D

E

F

G

## Tactics Tip: Successful Overt Close-range Visual Target Observation

During overt or disguised operative close-range visual target observation many agents openly approached the target, assuming that the enemy would take them for innocent locals. This bluff seemed to work when the mission involved inconspicuous personnel with an uncomplicated and convincing cover story. In early September 1944, for example, Margarethe Kelder and another female Dutch Resistance member walked nonchalantly into woods near Eindhoven and gathered mushrooms while unobtrusively observing a German flak battery. Eventually, they were confronted by suspicious German guards, but bags full of mushrooms and their unremarkable personas helped the women convince the guards of their innocence, and they were allowed to go on their way. Within hours PAN had fed this intelligence via taps on the civilian telephone net to 'Melanie', the OSS Mission in Eindhoven.

# Tactics Tip:
# Intelligence Gathering

Between 9 April and 5 September 1944, OSS inserted by parachute 30 two-person 'Sussex' operative teams into German-occupied France to assist the Allied campaign in Normandy. Their mission was to gather general intelligence, although occasionally some teams had to obtain precise pieces of information. On 10 August 1944, for example, the Americans requested information on a factory said to be near Le Bouchet that was suspected of manufacturing chemical weapons; two 'Sussex' teams redeployed to the factory and sent back valuable intelligence about it. Each team comprised an observer and a wireless-operator wearing civilian clothing and carrying civilian papers. Each team had a radio, for which they used a cipher with a flash code, a pre-arranged group of numbers, each of which stood for a particular word or phrase. The teams communicated with a dedicated receiver in England, Station Victor. The radio operator took with him, in addition to the radio, two batteries, two battery acid bottles, one generator and stand, and his/her codes, while the observer carried an S-phone. These teams radioed over 400 intelligence messages back to England.

observe enemy movements. During 45 days of activity, the team relayed 66 messages containing intelligence obtained by surveillance carried out by these guerrillas.

## Personal Reconnaissance

Another type of operative general intelligence-gathering mission was personal surveillance of terrain to identify possible sites for future operative insertion/extraction missions; this encompassed potential landing strips for Lysander aerial missions, as well as remote beaches for maritime missions. British Army Captain Conal O'Donnell from SOE Middle East, for example, parachuted into occupied Greece in late October 1943, to identify suitable locations within the mountainous Peloponnese where airstrips could be created, and to communicate this by radio to SOE's Cairo headquarters. These would be used by Lysander and Hudson aircraft to deliver arms to the local Greek Resistance. To accomplish this mission, he wandered the Peloponnese with his four-man team of radio operator, interpreter and two local partisan guards, attempting to find areas of flat grass fields suitable for a light plane to land upon, with unobstructed approaches and good drainage for use all year round. He also identified Lake Kaiafa as a suitable potential seaplane base after taking measurements of its length and width by pacing; in addition, using a sounding line dropped from a small rowing boat, he took soundings of the lake's depth; all this data he radioed to Cairo. In early 1944, moreover, having identified a suitable spot near Hanipanopoulou, he organized the local Resistance units to prepare a 914m (1000-yard) long grass strip by flattening the uneven surfaces, and removing boulders and large stones (see *Mission Profile: Recce on Rhodes*, p163).

## Capture of Documents and Equipment

Another method by which operatives obtained useful general intelligence was to view, copy or obtain enemy documents. All SOE agents were taught the necessary skills during their initial training courses. Having obtained sight of a document or possession thereof, the operative had a number of ways by which this

# Mission Profile:
# The Top Intelligence-Gatherers

Of the 30 OSS two-person Sussex teams inserted into enemy territory during 1944 to gather intelligence, the most effective was Team 'Jeanne'. Its two operatives parachuted into the French countryside near Orleans on 10 April 1944. The team sent 170 messages via its radio back to in England, of which 127 contained genuinely useful intelligence on enemy strengths and deployments.

# Sounding

Secret agents regularly employed sounding devices
thrown overboard from kayaks, dinghies, surf-boats
or midget-submarines to ascertain water depth along
shore-lines or in lakes. These devices comprised rope,
wire or chain, knotted or marked at one-fathom sections,
with a lead weight at the bottom.

could be exploited, depending on the situation and available resources. In the complete absence of any other feasible options, an operative could attempt to memorize the contents of a short document, and then recall it by writing it down again or sending a coded message back to his/her host country. Agents could also send Morse code summaries of longer documents, but it was difficult and time-consuming to convey long and complex data in this fashion.

## Copying

Most operatives preferred, if possible, to copy the documents and pass the copy onto the Allies through operative-couriers that were extracted by sea, air or land back to the United Kingdom. Operatives could make instant copies by photographing the documents with sub-miniature cameras like the Riga, which had the advantage that the enemy would probably never know that the item had been copied.

Alternatively, agents could steal the items for long enough to have them duplicated by a Mimeograph or Spirit Duplicator, before returning the items. This was obviously riskier than the previous option, but still offered the prospect of the enemy not knowing that any data had been compromised.

## Charm offensive

Another alternative approach to acquiring enemy documents was for the operative to exploit their

# Mission Profile: Recce on Rhodes

During 1941, Royal Navy Lieutenant-Commander Nigel Clogstoun-Willmott and Special Boat Section (SBS) Captain Roger Courtney undertook several recces of beaches in Rhodes, to facilitate a planned subsequent Allied amphibious assault. Inserted at night to the vicinity by submarine, the agents rowed their collapsible canoe for over a mile towards the beach; at 100m (109 yards) from the shore, Clogstoun-Willmott, in full wet-suit, then swam ashore. There he took measurements of the beach and the shallows but was surprised when an unexpected enemy patrol approached. Reacting coolly, he used the age-old technique of dropping silently to the ground and lying motionless, trying to breathe as quietly as possible as the patrol marched straight past him in the darkness. Finally, he signalled the canoe with his infrared lamp, got the expected response from the kayak, and used this to navigate himself as he swam back to the canoe.

masculine or feminine charms to strike up a physical relationship with an enemy service person or civilian employee. One form of this was the 'honey trap', in which after the operative had seduced the target and covertly recorded or photographed the incident, he/she would blackmail the victim into providing documents.

### Stealing

Finally, operatives could simply steal the documents, which was quick and straightforward but ran the obvious risk that the enemy would discover their disappearance. In some circumstances, however, this consequence was either an acceptable risk or else was unlikely to occur. During 1943, for example, OSS-Italy acquired substantial documentation through operative missions that combined audacity, bravado and naked force. It inserted 10-man agent teams onto remote Italian islands such as Stromboli, Lipari and Ponza, where through shows of force they overwhelmed and removed the token enemy garrisons, before carting off all available military documentation.

### Photographing documents

To assist agents in the effective photographic reproduction of enemy documents, SOE developed a microphotography capability. By using a top-performance camera

and ultra-fine-grain camera film, its scientists demonstrated that a foolscap German document could be photographed and the image reduced and reproduced on special film at a size of just ¹/₈th of an inch squared. Twenty such images could easily be fitted behind a stamp that was stuck on an envelope and simply posted. These capabilities, however, do not seem to have been pursued beyond these initial trials. SOE's technical 'boffins' also designed special devices to help operatives transport enemy documents without being detected.

One such device was an asbestos-lined pipe, inside which the operative hid captured enemy documents. The scientists also developed several document containers disguised within everyday items that were accessed via concealed screw-off tops; cleverly, the tops unscrewed clockwise rather than the normal anti-clockwise to prevent detection by enemy scrutiny.

In addition to intelligence gathering through acquiring or copying enemy documents, a few operative missions went much further – attempting to acquire data on enemy equipment by stealing it. In early December 1943, Danish Resistance operative Svend Otto Nielsen ('John'), apparently after receiving a request from England, covertly entered the German airfield at Kastrup, in Copenhagen's southeastern fringes,

# Minox Riga Sub-miniature Camera

**The Latvian factory VEF only produced the Minox Riga sub-miniature camera during 1937–43. It made an ideal spy camera, given its tiny size, light weight and advanced technical features, particularly its shallow minimum focus range. OSS operatives used these cameras on surveillance missions from 1942 onwards.**

with the assistance of a Danish civilian employee at the airbase, Knud Helge Hejl. Nielsen's mission was to steal a newly developed locating unit from a parked night fighter. Once inside the base, however, a German patrol spotted the intruders and arrested Hejl. 'John' fled and by crawling several kilometres on his hands and knees managed to escape, but only after he had killed an enemy sentry with his Welrod silenced pistol.

# Telephone Tap

**To create a telephone tap, an operative covertly spliced an additional phone wire onto both the original phone line's out and return wires; the operative would then run these new wires to a nearby covert OP, where they were connected to headphones or a telephone receiver.**

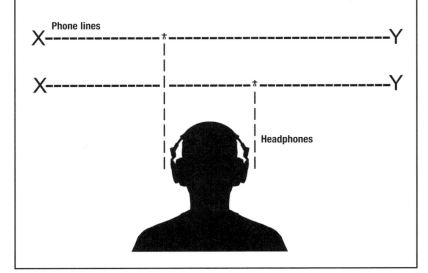

### Telephone-tapping

Operatives could also acquire general intelligence through telephone-tapping – intercepting or eavesdropping on enemy conversations. To accomplish this, the operative had to locate a section of enemy telephone wire in a remote location away from any scrutiny. The operative then spliced two additional phone wires, one each onto the phone line's two cables that formed the circuit carrying the information from the telephone exchange to the telephone receiver at the end of the line.

The operative would then lay the two spliced lines across the ground, under cover, to a suitable facility such as a shed or a hide/OP where they were connected to headphones, or to another telephone receiver and/or a recording device. During 1944, for example, the Dutch Resistance used the expertise of two activists employed at the Dutch Central Telephone Exchange to establish taps into the national civilian telephone network.

The Resistance also managed to use these taps as the basis of a clandestine communications system that allowed disparate groups to communicate with one another. On certain occasions, such as when advancing American units first reached the southern tip of the Limburg pan-handle on 12 September 1944, they discovered that with Resistance assistance they could communicate via these taps into the public telephone network with Resistance operatives in the rest of the country that was still under German occupation. After several days, the Germans severed any extant lines that ran from German-controlled territory into areas of the country liberated by the Allies.

The Resistance also established several taps on German military lines and communicated the valuable intelligence gathered to the Allied authorities in the United Kingdom. These capabilities, exploited by the four 'Jedburgh' teams inserted into the region, facilitated communication between the various Allied units landed during Operation 'Market-Garden', 17–25 September 1944.

## Mission-specific Intelligence-gathering

In addition to gathering general intelligence, agents also sought to acquire mission-specific information, either for missions to be carried out by regular forces or by themselves. Operatives might execute missions to gain data on terrain and enemy defences to facilitate a subsequent Allied amphibious assault or an airborne landing. During 1943–44, for example, 12-man Combined Operations Assault Pilotage Parties (COPPs) were inserted at night onto the beaches of northern France to obtain data about these landing sites; they measured the profile of both the shallows and the beaches, and took samples of beach composition.

The teams were inserted by small motor craft or midget submarines to the vicinity of the beach; they then rowed in collapsible canoes or swam; in either case each man wore a special COPP wet-suit The operatives took with them a sounding line – a weighted rope knotted at fathom intervals (one arm's-stretch being used to approximate a fathom), a Chinagraph pencil (attached to the

# COPP Wet Suit

**During 1943–44, British COPP agents employed special wet-suits to gather vital intelligence on the condition of enemy beaches in occupied France. The wet-suits contained vital water-proofed equipment such as buoyancy aids, an underwater writing tablet, a compass, pouches for beach samples, a pistol holster, knife scabbard and an ingenious underwater audio warning device known as a bong-stick.**

wetsuit by a short line to prevent it being dropped) and a matt-white slate for recording measurements, which could even be used underwater. They also took a fishing line on a reel attached to a brass rod (which was pushed into the sand) to measure the distance from the shore, and an auger tube for taking beach core samples.

### Patrick Leigh Fermor and Close-range Observation

Operatives also employed the techniques of close-range visual observation described above for mission-specific reconnaissance missions. On Crete in early April 1944, for example, after SOE agents Patrick Leigh Fermor and William

# Auger Tube

**Secret operatives employed an auger tube to obtain a sample core from a beach located behind enemy lines. After screwing the drill piece into the other core sections and fitting the handle, the agent then screwed the auger deep into the beach and then extracted it with the desired sample, which provided valuable intelligence for any planned future amphibious assault.**

# Tactics Tip:
# Clothing for Disguises

For any operative, but particularly for those attempting close-range visual intelligence gathering, a convincing disguise was essential. SOE's tailoring group undertook enormous efforts to equip their agents with clothing that was entirely appropriate to the given cover story, down to the tiniest detail. Clothing was made using European techniques, for example the back stud hole of a shirt collar was horizontal, not vertical as in the British fashion. Genuine clothing labels stolen by SOE agents were used to fabricate copies that were then sewn into agents' clothing. SOE also purchased the clothes of genuine refugees from Europe and used these to equip their agents.

Some clothing was also designed to aid operative survival. Some agents, for example, wore the SOE-designed evasion-assist string-vest (see illustration right). The vest could be unravelled and plaited to form a strong rope to aid escape.

### Make-Up
These services were augmented by SOE's make-up section. Using make-up experts recruited from the film industry, agents operating in the Mediterranean, for example, were shown how to apply special dyes and pigments to change their skin tones to aid their disguise as a local civilian.

Moss and two Cretan SOE operatives had arrived on the island by motor launch, they established themselves in a pre-arranged safe house located in a propitious yet audacious position – directly opposite the target, General Heinrich Kreipe's residence near the village of Knossos.

Next, Leigh Fermor dressed authentically as a local Cretan farmer, wearing an embroidered bolero top, a maroon-coloured cummerbund, a pair of corduroy riding-breeches and black boots (see *Tactics Profile: Clothing for Disguises*, above). The agent then undertook an overt close-

kidnap Kreipe in his car, while posing as German military policemen at an improvised checkpoint; the local Cretan resistance provided the enemy uniforms.

## Yelena Mazanik: Infiltrating Enemy Organizations

Another operative tactic to undertake mission-specific close-range visual target observation was to somehow get an agent to be accepted by the enemy and thus infiltrate them into the enemy organization.

In Minsk in Nazi-occupied White Russia, 20-year-old Yelena Mazanik, a local Partisan supporter, managed to obtain a job as a maid at the lavish household of Wilhelm Kube, the Nazi Commissar for White Russia. The detailed intelligence she gathered while working there made the planned assassination strike against the hated Nazi leader possible. Crucially, she discovered not only that Kube and his wife had separate beds within his private bed-chambers, but also that Kube himself slept nearest to the door. She also identified which parts of the household had additional security in the form of sentries. Having digested all this intelligence, the Partisan group organizing the strike decided that it was feasible for Yelena to smuggle a mine into the building and place it under Kube's mattress.

The details of the rest of this particular undercover story are covered in Chapter 6.

range visual reconnaissance of the area. This intelligence-gathering convinced the operatives that their original plan of getting into the residence was impracticable due to the number of guards present. Instead, the agents reformulated their plan and instead aimed to

The efforts to insert agents into enemy-occupied territory and subsequent organization, training and equipping of Resistance forces was all predicated on their undertaking violent action against Axis forces. Although passive resistance and propaganda had their place, since Winston Churchill had instructed SOE's first political head, Hugh Dalton, to 'set Europe ablaze', more active, aggressive activities would be required. SOE's *Partisan Leader's Handbook* of 1939 exhorted the reader to 'remember that your object is to embarrass the enemy in every possible way so as to make it more difficult to fight on the main front' by targeting his transport and communication systems.

Joseph Stalin demanded that the Soviet people 'fan the flames of the partisan movement in the enemy's rear, to destroy the enemy's logistic areas, and to destroy the German-Fascist scoundrels'. This would involve acts of sabotage – put simply, it meant blowing things up. Even Resistance movements such as *Milorg* in Norway, which was more concerned with forming

. . . . . . . . . . . . . . . . . . . . . . . . . . . . . . . .

**Sabotage could take many forms, including attacks on railway lines and vehicles. It involved the use of explosives, as well as simple techniques such as puncturing a vehicle's petrol tank.**

**Sabotage was a highly effective way of disrupting German communications and transport networks as well as tying up large numbers of troops in anti-Partisan and anti-Resistance actions.**

Sabotage

# *Milorg* Districts

Norway's resistance movement *Milorg* (*Militærorganisjonen* – Military Organization) was arranged into 14 regional districts under a Central Leadership Committee. By the time of liberation, *Milorg* had 40,000 men under arms, equipped and trained by SOE.

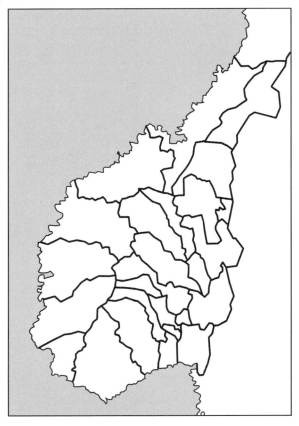

# Demolition Kit

**SOE produced all manner of explosive devices. Shown here are means of detonating explosives, including percussion caps, a dummy fog signal igniter, the time pencil fuse, detonating cord and a tripwire, which would operate a pull-switch that would set off the detonator.**

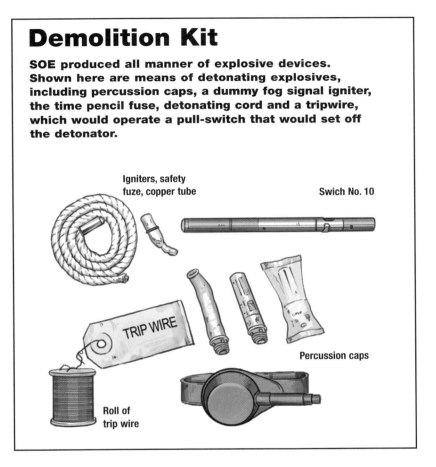

Igniters, safety fuze, copper tube

Swich No. 10

TRIP WIRE

Percussion caps

Roll of trip wire

an army-in-being for the liberation, or elements of the *Chetnik* movement in Yugoslavia, which seemed more interested in preparing for the coming reckoning with Tito's Partisans, recognized the need to undermine the German and Italian war effort. Indeed, in the aftermath of the Normandy landings, and particularly during the German Ardennes Offensive of December 1944 to January 1945, *Milorg* launched a concerted campaign against German rail and sea

# Explosive-Making Kit

This selection of explosives and detonators include a standard 1½lb charge of plastic explosive with detonating cord and time pencil attached, a set of delay action fuses, time pencils, a booby trapped wine bottle and tripwire.

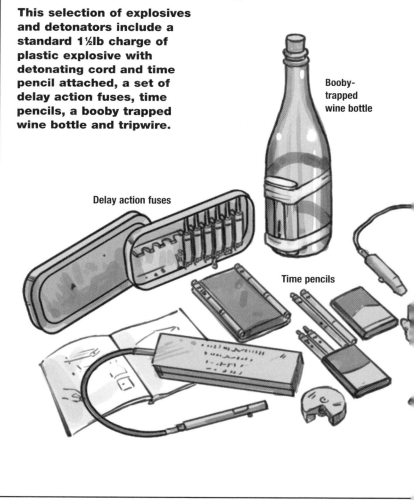

Booby-trapped wine bottle

Delay action fuses

Time pencils

communications to prevent the transfer of troops from Scandinavia to the crucial Northwest European front.

## Demolitions

Demolition training was a major part of the SOE training syllabus. Particular emphasis was put on anti-railway sabotage, and the West Highland Line in Scotland provided track and even a train for the agents to practise placing explosive charges and making their getaway. The agents worked with a wide range of explosives, such as gelignite and amatol. They were also taught how to make their own 'home-made' explosives using weed-killer or fertilizer. There was also a specialist three-week industrial sabotage course at STS 17 at Brickendonbury Manor, near Hertford, available to those who had finished the basic course. It was run by Lieutenant-Colonel George Rheam and aimed to really hone the agent's demolition and sabotage skills.

SOE's explosive of choice was plastic explosive (PE). PE, developed by the Nobel Company, had much to recommend it. It was safe, stable and malleable, and could be shaped as required. Even being struck by a bullet would not set it off. In fact, to set off PE and the other explosives you needed primer. In the case of PE this was a small electric charge or explosion. Traditionally, this was administered through the classic box-

Charge of plastic explosive

Detonator

Tripwire

and-plunger detonator. This had the advantage that the operator could set off the charge when he chose, which was particularly useful if the target was a moving vehicle. However, the closeness necessitated by line of sight, or the fact that the detonator was connected to the explosives by cord restricted the agent to the vicinity of the detonated device, which could throw up all sorts of problems.

### Fuses and Detonators

One solution was the Switch No 10, better known as the time pencil. This was a brass or aluminium tube, 12.7cm (5in) long, with a spring snout into which a detonator could be placed. Behind it was a copper section that contained a glass ampoule full of copper chloride. To activate it, all the agent had to do was crush the section containing the ampoule, which would release the copper chloride onto an iron wire. Then the safety strip should be removed and the time pencil would be armed. If the strip could not be taken out, it indicated that the wire was already broken and was resting on the safety strip. A new pencil should be selected.

If the pencil was functioning properly, removing the safety strip would arm it. The liquid from the broken ampoule would corrode the wire, which would break, releasing a spring that would fly into the percussion cap and set off the detonator. The time delay

# Detonating Plastic Explosive

**To explode a block of plastic explosive, a hole should be made, and a detonating cap attached to a length of detonating cord inserted. Some form of switch initiator, such as a time pencil, would be needed to set off the charge.**

was set by the type of pencil selected, based around the concentration of copper sulphide – the stronger it was the quicker it dissolved the wire. Some time prior to this moment the pencil, should have been inserted into the explosive and the saboteur made his getaway. The pencils were

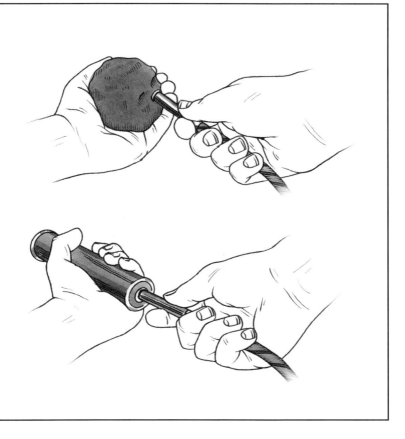

colour coded. Black was 10 minutes, red 30 minutes, green 5½ hours, yellow 12 hours and blue 24 hours. The delay were not as exact as, say, a clockwork timer, and there could be some minutes, even hours, leeway on the longer fuses (see *Equipment Profile: 'Pilchard' and the Time Pencils*, p181). Some agents particularly distrusted the shorter fuses, black and red, for this reason. Also, cold weather might lengthen the time and high temperatures shorten it. For high-value targets it was, therefore, recommended that two pencils, preferably from different batches, be used. One, at least, should go off, and ignite the explosive. Despite these limitations, time pencils were easy to use and had the added advantage of being silent, there being no fizz or hiss.

There are basically two methods of switch: the timed device, such as the time pencil; and instantaneous devices activated by switch. An example of this was the pressure pad, which responded to weight being placed on a hinged metal plate by releasing a striker to initiate a detonator. Also a pull switch could be used that would be initiated by a tripwire. There was also a pressure release switch, often known as an anti-disturbance switch, which was set off when a load on the device was moved.

# Attacking Railways

SOE was particularly keen to target the rail network. One device used against trains was a modification of the fog signal used to warn trains of danger ahead. However, the intention was to detonate the main charge some distance in front of the train. So that charge would be attached to the 'fog signal' switch by a length of detonator or instantaneous fuse (commercially known as Cordtex in the UK and Primacord in the USA). Alternatively, the saboteur might use a pressure switch under the rail, which was considerably more discreet and could be easily concealed. The ballast under the track had to cleared, a firm base

for the pressure pad provided and the gap between the pad bridged with an adjustable rod. This could be a difficult, fiddly job in the dark. Furthermore, the Germans would check the track regularly and also took to running a locomotive in front of trains carrying particularly important cargoes. One way round this was the Imber Switch which could be set to go off after a set number of trains (up to eight) had run over it.

## Derailing Trains

Trains were similarly appealing targets to Soviet Partisans. The explosives available were slightly less sophisticated but a 400g (1lb) charge of TNT (trinitrotoluene), which the Soviets considered 'fairly safe to work with' or Melinite (picric acid), which was considerably more unstable, would make short work of a stretch of railway track. The points on the track could be destroyed with two charges: one between the track and the narrow end of the points, the other at the narrow section itself. To demolish a frog (see *Rail Points*, p183), the cross track, the charge should be placed between the cross joint and the track. Failing that, the points mechanism could be destroyed with a sledgehammer or bent with a crowbar.

### Partisan Method

Indeed, the Soviet Partisan did not necessarily need explosives to deal

# Equipment Profile: 'Pilchard' and the Time Pencils

The problems with the fuses were well illustrated by the three-man 'Pilchard' SOE team dropped into France near Paris on the night of 5–6 May 1942. Their job was to attack the main Radio Paris transmitter at Allouis near Melun, which was being used to jam RAF signals traffic. They covered the 48km (30 miles) to the target over three nights, reconnoitred it and attacked on the night of 9–10 May. They were noisy enough to attract the attention of the sentries and came under fire. They had intended to press six-hour time pencils into their explosive charges before cutting their way into the station. However, they forgot to do this and so had to set the charges while under fire, before escaping. The time pencils turned out to be defective and they went off after only an hour and a half. As their after-action report recorded: 'if we had adhered to [our] plan – it would have been: Failure of a mission and the PILCHARD team in Paradise!' The mission was a success, however, putting the transmitter out of action for two weeks, while the team managed to escape safely into Spain.

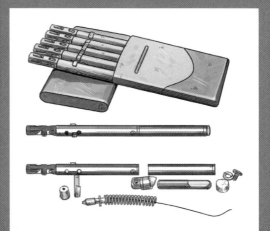

# Rail Sabotage Kit

A block of plastic explosive attached to the rail would be detonated by a pair of dummy fog signal igniters. Directly in front are a couple of pressure switches, including the Type 5 Imber Switch. In front of these are some plastic explosive, crimping pliers and detonating cord.

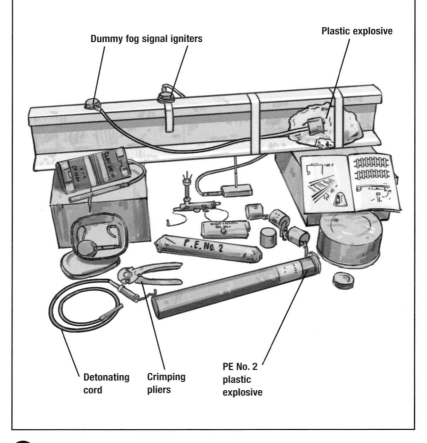

Dummy fog signal igniters

Plastic explosive

Detonating cord

Crimping pliers

PE No. 2 plastic explosive

# Rail Points

**The most vulnerable sections of railway track are the points. Explosives should be placed in the marked positions on switches, frogs and crossovers.**

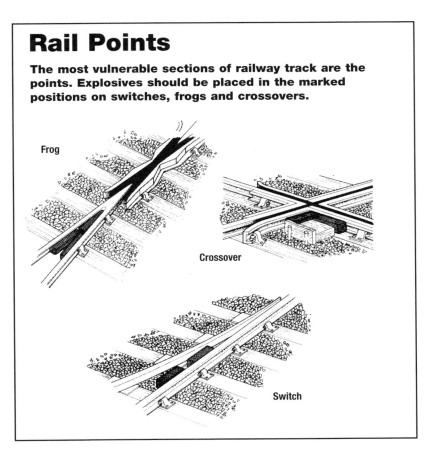

Frog

Crossover

Switch

with a moving train. There were four methods taught.

The first was to remove the nuts off both ends of a stretch of railway track and pull out the spikes from the railway sleeper. The track would now be free and could be moved 8–10cm (3–4in) to the side, and that should derail an oncoming train. The second was to remove the spikes from two or three sections of track without moving the bolts at the junctures; with a crowbar, move the tracks 10–12cm (4–5in) to the side and fix in the new position with the spikes. Again, derailment was unavoidable.

# Derailing a Train

The Soviet Partisans used four main methods of derailing trains. Some were relatively simple, such as removing the spikes holding the rails to the sleepers and shifting the rails, thereby disconnecting the lengths of track or undermining a length of track. A carefully positioned wedge could do the trick. Of course, if explosives were available, the task would be a lot less physically demanding.

SOE's so-called 'Polish charge' consisted of two ¾lb sticks of PE attached to fog signal igniters by a length of detonating cord. The oncoming train would set off the PE, removing about a metre length of track.

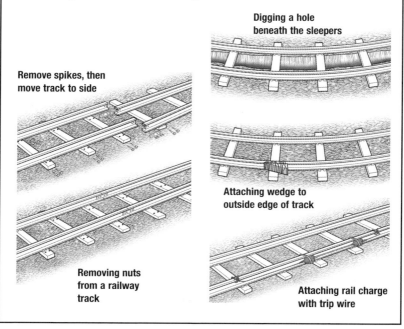

Digging a hole beneath the sleepers

Remove spikes, then move track to side

Attaching wedge to outside edge of track

Removing nuts from a railway track

Attaching rail charge with trip wire

The third method could be used on an embankment where the track turned sharply. The Partisans would then dig holes about half a sleeper wide and 50cm (19.6in) deep, under 15 or so sleepers of the outer track. This would leave the sleeper suspended in the air, and when the train moved over the undermined tracks, they would collapse, overturning the train.

The fourth method was the most complex and required some advanced preparation. It made use of a curve in the tracks. The Partisan had to make a straight wedge, 80cm (31in) long, 7cm (2.8in) thick and 5cm (1.9in) wide, out of a piece of dry hardwood such as oak. One side had to be cut to an angle and the wedge secured by wire to the outer track of the curve, so that the angled cut faced the oncoming train. When the train moved over the wedge, the leading wheel should have run up the wedge and so not make the turn, running on straight and leaving the tracks.

### Attacking Railway Bridges

It was not only the track that could be targeted, of course. There were, other, sometimes more valuable, targets. In their postwar analysis of guerrilla tactics, the Swiss reckoned that if the track was broken in one place on the main line, it might delay traffic by only about five to six hours. This was annoying and, on a large scale, possibly a major issue, but bridges were more obvious and serious choke points. Track was relatively easy to repair; a well-demolished bridge most certainly was not. The Soviets recommended targeting several parts of the bridge, particularly its lower parts, attaching a number of charges to spars, pillars, spans and girders, linked with detonating cord or a network of wires, if using an electric charge to set off the explosives. In this way, they could be set off simultaneously. It was better to overdo than underdo the charges, because if some of the bridge's pilings survived, it would aid the enemy's repair effort.

If the bridge was wooden, which was reasonably common in the more out-of-the-way places in Eastern Europe and the Balkans, the bridge could be burnt. Straw or twigs could be braided, doused in fuel, attached to the pilings and set alight.

### Sabotaging Rolling Stock

Similarly, rolling stock could be targeted. A kilogram of explosive carefully attached to an axle by wire would do the job on a steam engine, although it required time and care to put it in the right place.

When pressed for time, two 600g (1.3lb) demolition charges attached by rope could be hung over an axle. The rope needed to be short enough for the charge to touch the axle. However, the speed of application meant a large amount of explosive was used and might well achieve

# Mission Profile:
# The Gorgopotamos Bridge

The attack on the bridge over the Gorgopotamos River was an important SOE achievement in Greece. On the night of 25 November 1942, a team led by Monty Woodhouse of SOE attacked the immense viaduct across which ran the only rail link between Athens and Salonika in the north. The plastic explosive used took down two the bridge's spans and ensured that the only track between Greece and the rest of the Mediterranean was out of action. That line had been supplying about 48 trains a day to Rommel's troops fighting in North Africa.

relatively poor results. A charge could also be thrown into the engine's firebox.

If explosives were not available, the controls could be attacked with a sledgehammer or large-calibre bullets fired into the boiler. SOE suggested running off the water in the boiler and building up the fire. With no water to cool it, the firebox would eventually bend in the heat. On the actual wagons themselves, quite apart from explosives applied to the axles, abrasive substances could be added to the grease box for the axle.

Although no immediate result would be seen, the bearings would soon wear out. SOE even produced abrasive grease, made of ground carborundum, which when applied to

axle-bearings and similar vulnerable points could cause absolute havoc.

## Other Means of Sabotage

Yet, there were other, more subtle, ways of causing the Germans trouble on the railways.

Goods for the *Wehrmacht* were always moved in sealed trucks and labelled with a code indicating the truck's destination. When goods trains were formed or shunted, the trucks would be sorted out according to the destination codes. Fresh labels were issued at major interchange stations. All that had to be done to cause a little confusion and delay was to mix up a couple of labels so that the wrong material went to the wrong location, sights for tank guns to U-boat pens or whatever. It was the sort of error that would appear accidental and which was pretty much untraceable anyway.

Another tactic was for railway workers, without being too obvious about it, simply to 'go slow'. One German study reckoned that despite the bombing and the types of active sabotage described above, what really slowed up the railways in occupied Western Europe was 'the permanent attitude of non-cooperation and go-slow of the railway staff, even when they were not on strike, that made it impracticable to clear up enough of the mess for trains to run'.

## Operations Against Railway Transport

Irregular forces made a number of concerted efforts against the rail transport network of German-occupied Europe. As mention above, *Milorg* launched a campaign against the Norwegian rail network as the Germans tried to move some of the 15 divisions they held in Norway to the continent to support the Ardennes Offensive in early 1945. More than 1000 men, trained and equipped by SOE, cut the tracks and destroyed 10 bridges.

To add to the confusion, Gunnar Sønsterby and SOE's Oslo Gang blew up the five-storey building housing the German railway administration in Oslo, burying their records in the rubble. Rail traffic was delayed, on average, by a month.

More famously, however, the *Maquis* attacked the French rail network prior to and during the D-Day landings and the subsequent campaign to disrupt the reinforcement of German forces attempting to contain the Normandy beach-head. The 2nd SS Panzer Division *Das Reich* was ordered north from the South of France on 7 June, D+1. No fewer than 800 acts of rail sabotage forced it to move by road, a journey that should have taken about three days. However, subsequent action by the Resistance, and a pause by elements of the division to massacre 642 French civilians at Oradour-sur-Glane, meant that it actually took *Das Reich* 16 days to reach the front.

Soviet Partisans were similarly active. Amongst the most impressive actions was the massive coordinated attack against German railway traffic in the summer and autumn of 1943. The operation, codenamed 'Rail War', involved 541 Partisan detachments, 96,000 personnel in all. It primarily targeted the rail networks in Belorussia and central Russia supporting the German Army Group Centre. It opened in August 1943, although some smaller operations had taken place in support of the Kursk counter-offensive in July.

Although the full paralysis of the network was not achieved, the

# Placing Demolition Charges

**The Soviets recommended putting numerous charges around the positions indicated here. If in a hurry, and unable to make careful calculations, they recommended using multiple large charges (20–30kg/44–66lbs) on the lower parts of the spans, detonated simultaneously.**

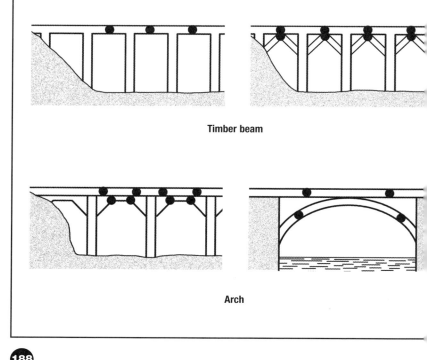

Timber beam

Arch

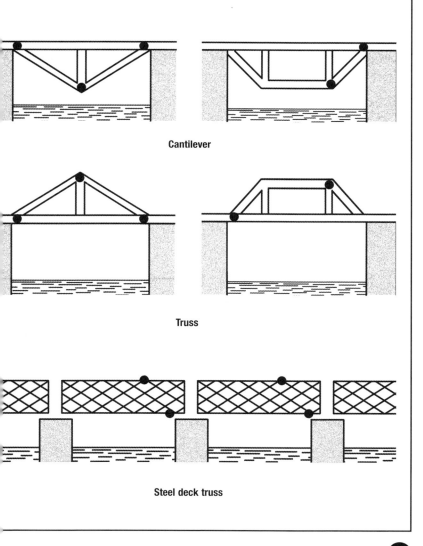

Cantilever

Truss

Steel deck truss

# Types of Bridge

**Different types of bridges have different vulnerable points, and it is these that need to be targeted. Clearly, on major bridges, this would be a complicated task, and more than likely, the bridges would be heavily guarded. Nonetheless, these vital choke points were tempting targets and their destruction, even temporarily, could be of real value to the Allied war effort.**

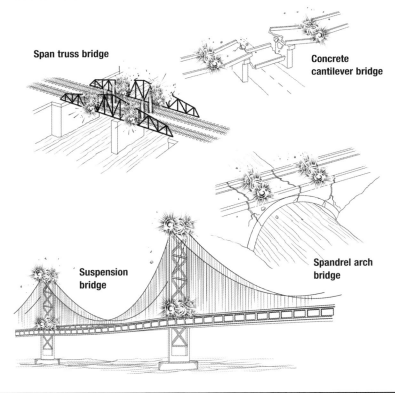

Span truss bridge

Concrete cantilever bridge

Suspension bridge

Spandrel arch bridge

Germans noted that rail traffic slowed considerably through August and around the Eighteenth Army area near Leningrad it virtually ceased. Lack of explosives meant momentum was lost, and some Soviets thought the operation, in targeting just the rails and not the trains, had not been been well thought through.

As a result, Operation 'Concert' was launched as a follow-up in September. It involved more than 100,000 Partisans. This time, they went for both the rails and the trains and consequently there was greater material effect. Once again, Soviet Partisans had demonstrated the strategic usefulness of irregular forces.

## Attacking Road Traffic

Rail traffic, of course, was not the only method of communications that could be targeted. Road networks are vulnerable and modern armies rely very heavily on motor transport. SOE provided miniature caltrops, four-pointed metal spikes, which could be showered on roads, bursting tyres and causing all sorts of problems for motorized columns.

Mines could be used, either set of by pressure or triggered at an appropriate moment. Even more simply, trees and telegraph poles could be felled across roads to create a temporary roadblock or facilitate an ambush. As with railways, road bridges made particularly effective targets. Only a

few pounds of plastic or other explosive would do the job on most country bridges.

The vehicles themselves could be targeted. A small charge of explosive would wreck the front axle, and OE came up with a small thermite bomb that was perfect for torching cars and trucks. More simply, an early SOE pamphlet recommended knocking a hole in the bottom of the petrol tank and setting the escaping fuel alight. If that was impractical, there was always the old movie stand-by of putting sugar in the petrol tank. Tyres could be slashed. Petrol stores themselves made a tempting target.

## Attacking Communications Networks

Telegraph and telephone wires and electric power cables were vulnerable to attack and also very accessible to saboteurs. The poles supporting the telegraph wires could be cut or blown. Trees could be felled into the wires. When cutting the wires, it was worth removing as much as possible. Cut wires were easily traced, so the Soviets suggested pulling the telegraph wires together near the insulators, using another piece of wire to create a short-circuit. Such damage was deemed more difficult to detect.

Even more simply, a strong rope tied to a heavy weight or small rock could be tossed over the wires to wrap around them. A sharp pull of

# Road Bridge Observation

**If a bridge was to be targeted or a convoy attacked, it was vital to conduct careful reconnaissance first. Regularity of road traffic and guard routines (if any) needed to be studied, from a suitable vantage point. A demolition expert might well be able to estimate size and suitable locations for explosives charges from a distance.**

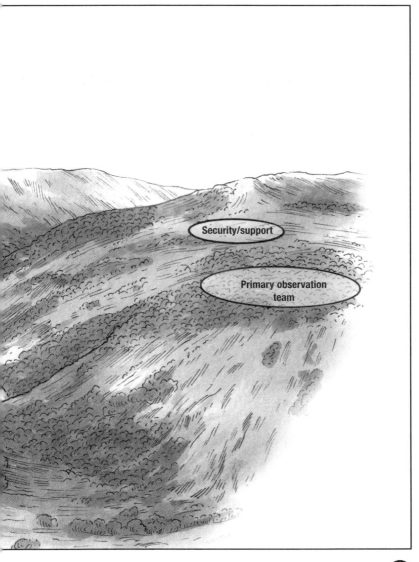

# Roadside Bomb

There were essentially two straightforward methods for the passive use of explosives against enemy vehicles: the roadside bomb or stake mine triggered by a tripwire device; or uncontrolled pressure-sensitive landmine. Both weapons might well constitute a considerable danger to the local civilian population.

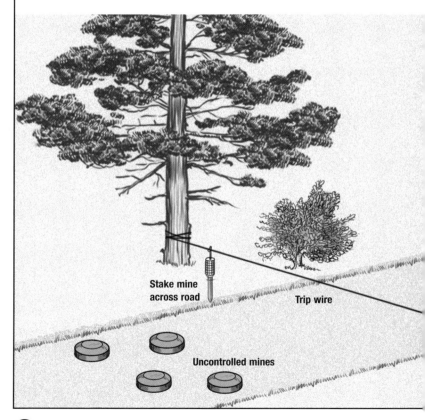

Stake mine across road

Trip wire

Uncontrolled mines

Enemy truck

# Sabotaging a Vehicle

**All sorts of options were available to operatives sabotaging enemy vehicles. Caltrops could be laid in large numbers on roads or placed immediately in front of the tyre of a parked car. Tyres could be slashed. Sugar could be added to the petrol tank or the tank itself punctured.**

**Caltrops**

**Putting sugar in petrol storage**

the rope ought to be enough to snap the wires. It was easier if attempted at the mid-point between the poles. If a buried cable was discovered, it was best to make several concealed breaks in it. Actually damaging the wire was quite easy; it just needed to be bent in the same place a number of times until the metal core inside the insulation was broken.

Junction boxes could be targeted and, perhaps more irritating than just destroying them, someone with specialist knowledge could mix the cables and wires. This could cause wrong numbers to be dialled or even open up the network to

eavesdropping by the Resistance. It is also worth noting that damaging wire communications also forced the Germans to increase their wireless traffic, which was more vulnerable to interception and decoding by the Allies.

## Attacking Sea Transport

Sea traffic could only really be disrupted by targeting the actual ships involved, although there was clearly scope for sabotage in ports and dockyards.

The most effective means of dealing with a ship was by a saboteur attaching explosives to the hull. The British-designed limpet mine Mark 1 was attached to

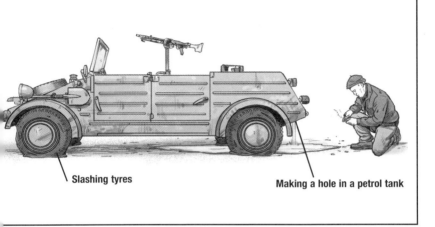

Slashing tyres

Making a hole in a petrol tank

a ship by six magnets. The resulting explosion would produce a hole impossible to patch. The mine took a coloured fuse based on an acid bulb to determine the delay. The colour-coded system produced delays from four-and-a-half hours to five-and-a-half days with a number of other options in between at a water temperature of 4.4° Celsius (40° Fahrenheit). The mines were attached to the ship about 60cm (2ft) below the waterline with a specially designed placing rod.

The main problem was actually approaching the ship, as harbours were usually very well-guarded places. The simplest way of making a silent approach was to use a canoe or kayak either single or double with conventional paddles. SOE produced a canvas folding canoe, the Folboat. These were used by a small group of Royal Marines to attack shipping in Bordeaux harbour on the River Gironde in December 1942. Norwegian SOE men also used canoes to attack German shipping in Norwegian waters in conjunction with naval MTBs during the Vestige operations of 1943 and 1944.

Max Manus, also of SOE's Norwegian section, simply used a rubber dingy in his attack on the ship SS *Donau* in January 1944 (see Chapter 3).

Although SOE never made use of frogmen, the Italians launched a number of operations, usually in conjunction with *Maiale* human torpedoes, that severely damaged the battleships HMS *Queen Elizabeth* and *Valiant* in Alexandria Harbour in December 1941.

## Industrial Sabotage

Transport and communication networks were not the only targets available. Modern total war requires vast industrial output to keep armies in the field. The Germans quickly put the industries of the countries that they occupied into the service of the *Reich*'s war-machine (see below *Mission Profile: Self-Sabotage at Peugeot*, p201).

George Rheam of SOE's Station XVII was the master of industrial sabotage. He taught his pupils to ask themselves a number of questions and thereby, economically and efficiently, bring a factory to a standstill. Look at the tool or machine. Was its base made of cast iron? If so, hit it with a hammer – cast iron tends to fracture easily. Has the machine some irreplaceable part? If so, break it or remove it. Can you use or programme the machine to destroy itself or those next to it? Then use it accordingly. Remember also if the machine wrecked can easily be fixed by cannibalizing those next to it, then you must destroy them all.

# Sabotaging a Telegraph

**A simple means of sabotaging telegraph wire was to cut down the poles. The wires themselves could be brought down by felling trees directly into them. Repairs could be made more difficult by installing booby traps.**

# Resistance in Normandy

**The Anglo-American invasion of North West Europe in June 1944 was much facilitated by the actions of the French Resistance both in Normandy and deeper into France. Local *Maquis* groups, alerted to the imminence of the invasion, targeted German communications and transport networks, hampering the Germans' ability to respond and reinforce quickly.**

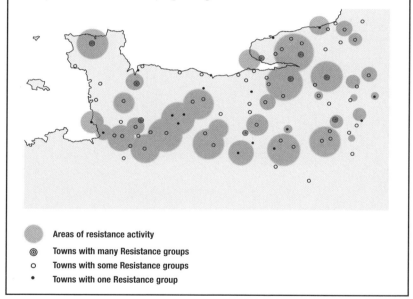

⬤ Areas of resistance activity
◎ Towns with many Resistance groups
○ Towns with some Resistance groups
● Towns with one Resistance group

SOE produced a number of useful devices. Explosives and abrasive materials have already been discussed but burning the factory down was an option and might even be considered to be an accident. SOE produced a number of incendiary devices, including: the 0.79kg (1.75lb) Mk II Firepot; the 1.1kg (2.5lb) Thermite Bomb; and the smallest incendiary that incorporated its own delay, the Pocket Time Incendiary

Mk II B, a 99g (3.5oz) device, which could produce a white-hot flare-like flame for a minute. Put in the right place in the vicinity of combustible material, it could be devastating.

### Partisan Method

The Soviets, as ever, came up with a more rough-and-ready method of committing arson. They suggested taking about 100 matches – about two matchboxes' worth – and spreading them out on a cheesecloth or even a regular rag, punctured all over to let in air. Then the cloth should be doused with oil and a hemp wick put into it. Hemp wick burns at 2cm (0.78in) a minute, so agents had to calculate the necessary length.

Put a piece of cloth or oakum soaked in oil around the wick, light it and move away. As the Partisan manual said: 'The fire will start in your absence.' The Soviets had an alternative: put a box of matches in a can of floor wax or shoe polish. Ignite and then retire. Given the rather erratic nature of such an incendiary device, they suggested that agents experiment with the mixture before they use it operationally.

## Operation 'Gunnerside'

It is quite clear that sabotage undertaken against the Axis transport and communication networks had an important strategic effect. The effect of SOE, OSS, resistance and Partisan industrial sabotage, however, seems less tangible. It caused irritation and delay and added to general sense of unease

# Mission Profile:
# Self-Sabotage at Peugeot

One of the remarkable achievements of SOE in France was persuading the Peugeot Company to sabotage its own factory. SOE agent Henri Rée persuaded one of the senior members of the Peugeot family that rather than suffer the damage that the RAF might cause, he should ensure that his family's factory struggled to meet German production requirements. As a result, his factory made very little contribution to the Nazi war effort and escaped the worst depredations of the RAF.

felt by the occupiers. However, it is worth ending this chapter with a mention of the action that SOE's excellent official historian M.R.D. Foot described thus: 'If SOE had never done anything else 'Gunnerside' would have given it claim enough on the gratitude of humanity.'

Operation 'Gunnerside' was the attack on the Norsk Hydro Heavy Water Plant at Vemork near Rjukan in central Norway. Heavy water is an effective moderator of neutrons in an atomic pile and so, when the British discovered that the Germans were increasing production at Vemork, it was an indication that they were working on an atomic bomb. A first attack by British paratroopers, named Operation 'Freshman', was launched in late 1942 but failed when the military gliders crashed short of their destination.

However, a six-man party of Norwegian SOE men, all veterans of Station XVII, led by Joachim Rønneberg, was dropped by parachute in appalling weather in February 1943. Dressed in British uniform, the team attacked the plant on the night of 26–27 February 1943. Substantial damage was done to the German atomic bomb project and the entire team escaped safely. The raid was followed by Allied bombing raids, forcing the Germans to move operations elsewhere.

# Partisan Arson Technique

1. **Empty the contents of two match boxes (about 100) onto a cloth and spread them out.**
2. **Puncture the cloth all over to let in air.**
3. **Douse the cloth with oil.**
4. **Put a hemp wick into it. (Hemp wick burns at 2cm (0.8in) a minute, so calculate the necessary length.)**
5. **Put a piece of cloth or oakum soaked in oil around the wick.**
6. **Light the wick and move away.**

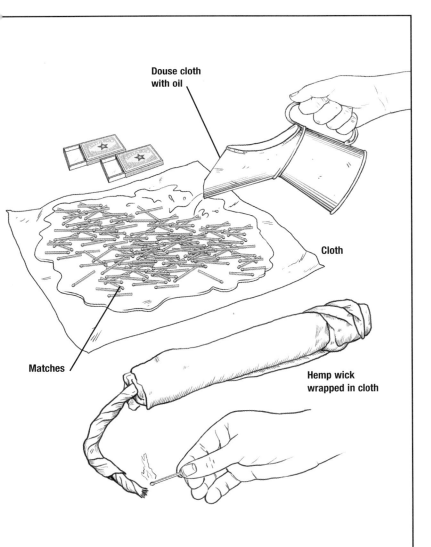

Douse cloth
with oil

Cloth

Matches

Hemp wick
wrapped in cloth

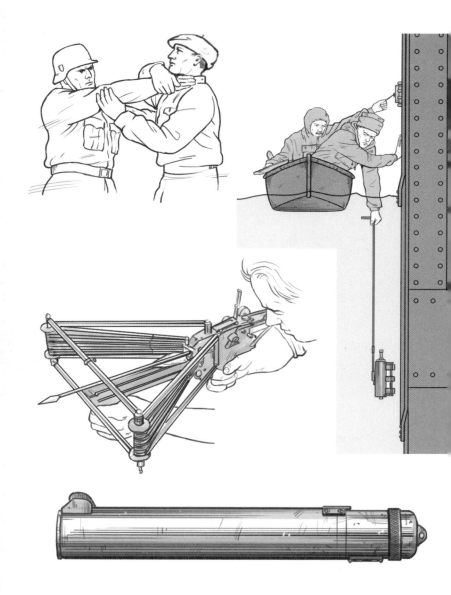

The ultimate purpose of most operative missions was to engage the enemy behind the latter's lines. As well as striking the enemy through sabotage, operatives also sought to take on enemy personnel – to kill or capture them – as well as destroy or damage their equipment and infrastructure. Operatives did this through engaging in three types of operations: by carrying out assassinations; by conducting ambushes and raids; and through executing guerrilla warfare.

Many operative missions aimed to kill senior enemy personnel through assassination. Secondly, many agents, usually acting in small groups, engaged enemy forces in ambushes and raids. Finally, operatives trained, organized and assisted local Resistance groups to conduct guerrilla warfare against the enemy. This chapter will examine the various ways, discussed above, in which operatives engaged in combat against enemy forces.

## Assassination

A number of operative missions aimed to assassinate key enemy leaders – termed high-value targets –

**6**

**Although not primarily deployed for combat, agents and Resistance fighters needed to use violence as part of their clandestine campaign against the occupiers.**

Combat

• • • • • • • • • • • • • • • • • • • • • • • • • • •

**In addition to unarmed combat, secret operatives engaged the enemy using various devices: limpet mines; sleeve pistols as an emergency weapon; and crossbows for silent assassination.**

because with a relatively modest outlay in terms of resources, and courage, agents could exert a high psychological impact on the enemy. Operatives undertook assassination missions in a variety of ways, utilizing a range of weapons. One obvious approach was to strike the target from a distance, with a long-range weapon such as a sniper's rifle. Other operatives got up close to the target, using surprise and concealment, to use a short-range weapon such as a pistol, which was much easier to conceal.

A long-range assassination strike using sniper's weapons afforded the advantages of not having to approach the victim, being able to tee-up the strike without haste, and of facilitating escape and extraction. That said, stand-off assassination brought with it several disadvantages: it was not easy to secure a kill with the first round, even for a skilled marksman (most agents were not marksmen), and operatives would rarely get a second shot; it was not easy to identify the correct target at a distance; the target might become obscured by other individuals present at the scene; and the weapon, being long and bulky, was hard to conceal and hampered escape/evasion. The sniper's rifle was one of the assassination methods considered under the 1944 SOE planning for Operation 'Foxley', the intended assassination of Hitler.

## Short-range Attacks

Because of these disadvantages, therefore, virtually all Allied operative assassination strikes were undertaken at short range. This approach had three main advantages: because the weapon employed was small and light, such as a pistol or a knife, it could be easily concealed on the operative's person, making detection less likely; the strike's short range maximized the chances of killing the target and minimized the risk of collateral damage to innocent bystanders; and in escaping the scene, the operative could retain the weapon without hindering his speed or mobility. That said, close-range assassination posed considerable risks to the agent: by having to get close to the target, the operative ran major risks of being detected and thus thwarted in the strike and even captured; it made the initial phases of extraction riskier as well; and – as discussed in Chapter 4 – it required accurate intelligence to be gathered first.

During these close-range assassination strikes operatives employed a number of different approaches and techniques to get close to the victim. Getting into an enemy barracks or compound was the most challenging approach and was rarely attempted. When it was attempted, operatives typically used guile and concealment to infiltrate into the target area rather than by

# *Maquis* Resistance Fighter

Here is a typical Resistance operative, dressed in local civilian clothing, equipped with a Browning .35 calibre pistol, probably part of a batch of weapons supplied to the local group by parachute from an Allied aircraft sortie. The operative also possesses a stiletto-style dagger, which could be concealed up a sleeve or tucked into a boot, if required.

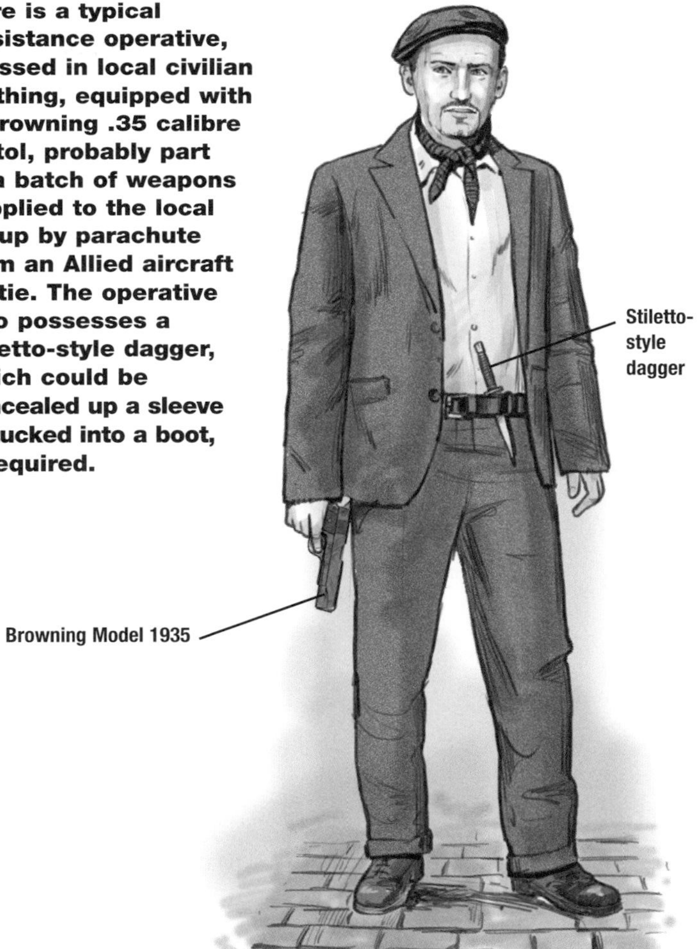

Stiletto-style dagger

Browning Model 1935

207

applying outright force. The Soviet Partisan Yelena Mazanik, for example, got a job as a maid in Wilhelm Kube's Minsk residence, permitting her subsequently to assassinate him while he slept. Many operatives chose to strike their victim out in the open, often when they were travelling, so that the operative could mingle unobtrusively among the throng of ordinary civilians going about their daily business.

As described in *Mission Profile: Assassination – Target Heydrich* (p234), the two SOE-trained Czech operatives who assassinated SS-General Reinhard Heydrich in Prague did so when the target was travelling in his own personal car – a tactic also employed when SOE operatives kidnapped General Heinrich Kreipe on Crete. Norwegian agents employed similar tactics when they followed in a stolen car the target, Norwegian collaborator Ivar Grande, as the latter cycled home, and assassinated him. In other missions operatives attempted to approach the victim by stealth. In an earlier attempted strike on Grande, an

# SOE Pistols

Ballester-Mollina 0.45

Llama Mark V 0.38 ACP

**From 1943 onwards, many SOE operatives carried either the Ballester-Mollina 0.45 or the Llama Mark V 0.38 ACP pistols. SOE often preferred using foreign-manufactured weapons such as these because, if the devices were captured, this alone might not alert enemy intelligence to the presence of an SOE team in the area.**

# .35 Cal Sleeve Pistol

**The obvious advantage of a specially designed weapon such as the Sleeve Pistol was that it was easily concealed; it also retained its cartridge on firing. That said, however, its effective range was just a few feet and it was a one-shot weapon.**

Trigger

Grip for unscrewing end cap

Silencer tube

Muzzle

Locking and cocking lugs

operative silently rowed across a nearby lake, but was deterred when the target's dog began barking. In maritime milieu, of course, operatives could approach the target silently in kayaks, midget submarines or even just by swimming. In September 1942, for example, Australian operatives silently kayaked their way into Singapore harbour at night to sink seven enemy vessels using limpet mines.

## Special Weapons

In order to carry out short-range assassinations, operatives employed various weapons including small arms (pistols and submachine guns), explosive weapons (grenades, mines and limpet mines) and poisons

(chemical agents and biological toxins). Many operative close-range assassinations employed pistols. During 1943–45 many SOE agents carried either the Spanish-manufactured Llama Mark V 9.6mm (0.38in) ACP or the Argentinean-produced Ballester-Mollina 11.4mm (0.45in) pistols (both variants of the American 1911-model Colt 45), which could kill a victim with just one close-range shot. The other advantage of pistols was that they could be easily concealed, making it more likely that the operative could complete the mission and escape successfully. To augment the ability of an operative to utilize a pistol without being detected, several countries manufactured special

# Equipment Profile:
# A Unique Disguised German Pistol

It was not just the British, with weapons such as the Welpipe and Welwoodbine, who produced pistols designed to look like an innocuous everyday item. Late in the war, for example, troops of the US XX Corps discovered a unique German pistol that had been made to resemble a black swastika-bedecked belt buckle. The front face of the buckle could be dropped down and when a button was pushed, the

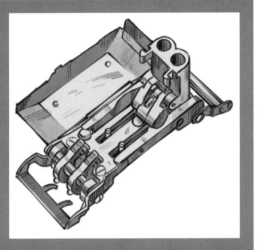

pistol flipped out, pointing forward. The weapon was a short two-barrelled 8.1mm (0.32in) pistol. By pressing two further buttons, the weapon could fire a single shot from each barrel.

pistols that were concealed within, or resembled, an everyday object. SOE produced the Welwand Sleeve pistol, a small single-shot, tube-shaped weapon that the operative kept up his sleeve. When the operative was within range of the intended victim (within 3m [10ft]), he/she would shake it down the

sleeve until it was in the hand (where it was almost undetectable); the operative would fire it by pressing down with the thumb on the trigger device positioned at the weapon's top. The cartridge remained in the weapon, so there was no tell-tale evidence left behind of a weapon being fired.

While several dozen SOE operatives took the Welwand with them to Nazi-occupied Europe, there is no documentary evidence describing when and how it was used; most probably, operatives employed it as a last resort in order to avoid capture; nevertheless, some of them were captured, and later died in captivity. SOE also designed other concealed pistols, such as the Welwoodbine, a cylindrical device disguised within a genuine European cigarette paper, and the Welpipe, a single-shot 5.56mm (0.22in) pistol concealed within a smoking pipe.

# SOE Crossbows

**To maintain secrecy, silent, silenced or suppressed weapons were often used by operatives on assassination missions. Available to SOE's agents were two specially designed miniature crossbows, 'Li'l Joe' and 'Big Joe'.**

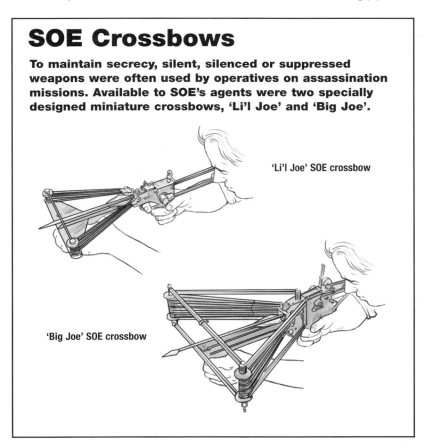

'Li'l Joe' SOE crossbow

'Big Joe' SOE crossbow

See *Equipment Profile: A Unique Disguised German Pistol* (p210) for a description of a gun disguised as a Swastika belt-buckle.

### Silent Weapons

Another preferred type of weapon employed by operatives for close-range assassination strikes was the silent weapon or silenced/suppressed versions of regular weapons; the lack or limitation of noise helped the operative preserve secrecy. SOE designed a number of specialized silent weapons for its field agents. These included two types of crossbow, named 'Li'l Joe' and 'Big Joe', available to agents on request via the SOE weapons and equipment catalogue. SOE operatives were also supplied with small knives or stickers. Many of the latter were specially-designed to be housed inside an innocuous common-day object like a pencil or a quill pen.

While desirably quiet, knives were not commonly used for assassination attempts because the agent would

# Quill Pen

**A sticker was essentially a long, pencil-like dagger. Operatives carried such weapons as a last resort, typically to be employed when confronted by a suspicious guard or official. To maintain secrecy, many stickers were designed to be housed in a common-day objective, such as a quill pen or pencil.**

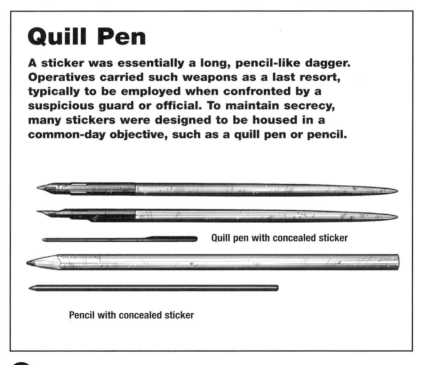

**Quill pen with concealed sticker**

**Pencil with concealed sticker**

# Sten Mk II with Silencer

**The Silenced Sten gun was often the weapon of choice for SOE and local Resistance groups on assassination missions. Crudely manufactured but resilient, it generated a high rate of fire and was employed at relatively short range, with its relative lack of noise on firing helping to maintain secrecy and surprise.**

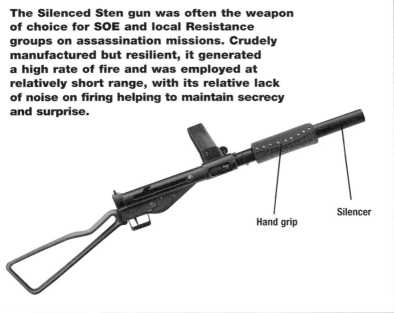

**Hand grip**

**Silencer**

have to get within arm's-length of the victim. Agents did often use them, however, to kill a target that could easily be approached with stealth and surprise, such as a lone sentry, often as part of an ambush or a raid. Operatives also used knives silently to finish off stunned or incapacitated enemy personnel, again most typically a guard.

Beyond these offensive operations, operatives also employed knives for self-defence, in particular to avoid being captured. In June 1941, for example, Dorothea McCloud ('Coco') was in the middle of planting plastic explosives in a railway signal box in Northern France when she walked around the side of the box and bumped into a German sentry; before the sentry could reach for his sidearm, 'Coco' whipped out her SOE-issue knife and stabbed him to death.

# De Lisle Commando Carbine

Silencer barrel

Magazine

**A rare, but much-prized, piece of SOE equipment, the de Lisle .45 ACP calibre suppressed bolt-action carbine was a compact weapon that also helped maintain secrecy through its relative lack of noise when fired.**

## Suppressed Weapons

OSS and SOE operatives, moreover, often employed either suppressed versions of their standard weapons or specially designed suppressed weapons. Agents often employed the suppressed version of the 9mm (0.35in) Sten sub-machine gun for close-range assassinations. The standard (non-suppressed) Sten was much favoured by operatives,

in general. It was light, simple to use, easy to maintain, robust, resilient, and, with its 32-round magazine, could produce a high rate of fire (300–500rpm) at typical ranges of 10–100m (9–91 yards). It was an area suppression weapon rather than a pin-point one, and hence was not suitable if the target needed to be picked out from a crowd of non-combatants. This basic weapon

# Welrod Silent Pistol

Silencer barrel

The Welrod was SOE's principal, purposely designed, single-shot suppressed pistol, made in 0.32" (7.65mm) or 9mm calibre versions. It was light, easy to conceal and quiet to fire, but needed considerable skill in firing technique to obtain accuracy beyond short range.

Detachable magazine inside hand grip

was also favoured because it was straightforward to manufacture – indeed SOE parachuted in barrels while local Resistance groups often locally manufactured the other parts. The most famous example of an SOE assassination using a Sten Gun was that against Heydrich.

Another silenced weapon employed by operatives was the de Lisle 11.4mm (0.45in) ACP calibre suppressed bolt-action carbine. Although only produced in small numbers, SOE agents prized it because it was not only compact but was also one of the quietest Allied weapons when firing.

But SOE's most commonly employed silenced weapon was the suppressed version of the Sten (the Mark II-S and Mark VI-S). Introduced in June 1943, this rapid-fire weapon could only be heard and identified at a range of under 200m (656ft), and the suppressor also eliminated the muzzle flash, helping to maintain secrecy when mounting night-time operations. Its main drawback was that the suppressed barrel tended to overheat quickly, so operatives fired the weapon in short bursts. Despite this, SOE agents used it on many close-range assassinations. On 12 December 1944, for example, an agent fired an entire 32-round magazine from his suppressed Sten at Norwegian collaborator Ivar Grande as the latter cycled home from work, after two operatives had followed the target in a stolen car; unsurprisingly, Grande died instantly.

British Operatives also employed the Welrod, a specially designed suppressed 8.1mm (0.32in) calibre pistol. With some 600 produced, the Welrod was issued to agents during 1943 and 1944. During October 1943, SOE planned what was known as Operation 'Execution Month', in which dozens of key German civilian leaders were to be assassinated using the Welrod; fear of German reprisals led to the operation's cancellation, however. In the last week of January 1944, moreover, SOE operatives in Norway, Denmark, Belgium, and France assassinated dozens of Gestapo officials and informants, as well as other Nazi collaborators using several dozen Welrod pistols and dozens of Suppressed Stens.

On 17 December 1944, Danish operative Henning Roge ('Max') attempted to assassinate Gestapo informant Henry Meister in a village near Aalborg using a Welrod. Although 'Max' successfully hit the target in the stomach, Meister managed to shoot back, killing the agent. American agents from the OSS employed a similar weapon – the HDMS 5.56mm (0.22in) Silenced Pistol.

## Explosives

Another preferred method, employed by secret operatives to conduct close-range assassination, was the use of explosive weapons, such as grenades, bombs, mines and other improvised explosive devices (IEDs). Operatives often took grenades with them for assassination missions, either as the principal attack device or as an ancillary to a main strike weapon such as a suppressed Sten or Welrod. Grenades were small and light, easy to conceal, had some range (10–25m [30–80ft]) and inflicted damage on a wide area. Consequently, they could injure or kill up to a dozen enemy personnel at one go.

When Jozef Gabcík stepped forward to assassinate Reinhard Heydrich, for example, he found to his horror that his Sten had jammed; luckily, his co-attacker had brought with him a modified British Type 73 anti-tank hand grenade; reacting

# Type 73 Anti-Armour Hand Grenade

**SOE employed the British Type 73 anti-armour hand grenade as a devastating and easily concealed short-range weapon to assassinate German 'high-value' targets, as well as during sabotage attacks. The most infamous victim of this device was SS General Heydrich.**

Bakelite safety cap

N.G. 73.A.T Mk.1. M.B.Co. 40.

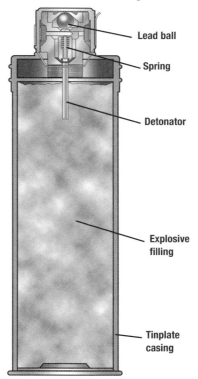

Lead ball

Spring

Detonator

Explosive filling

Tinplate casing

# Tactics Tip:
# Assassination with a Mine

One famous example of an operative assassination using a mine was carried out by Byelorussian Partisans working with the Soviet Secret Police (the NKVD). During 1942, these organizations developed a plan to eliminate Wilhelm Kube, the brutal Nazi Commissar for White Russia.

Fortuitously, a covert Resistance activist, the well-built 20-year-old Yelena Mazanik, had managed to obtain a job as a maid at Kube's lavish household in Minsk. On 22 September 1943, Yelena smuggled a small magnetic mine, which had previously been set to go off in 24 hours' time, into the house, hidden in her handbag. Knowing that this would be searched as she approached Kube's private quarters, she went to the toilet and there hid the bomb in her undergarments; her physical bulk helped conceal the object.

Next, by distracting the duty guard outside Kube's private quarters with the offer of a cup of coffee waiting for him downstairs, Yelena gained access to Kube's quarters. Rushing into the bedroom, she placed the mine under his mattress and dashed back out just in time before the guard returned from his coffee-break. That evening Kube went to bed and some hours later the mine exploded, seriously wounding him; he died of his wounds shortly afterwards. The successful assassination, however, provoked SS troops to execute 1000 Minsk citizens.

quickly to this unforeseen setback, Josef threw his grenade and injured Heydrich, who subsequently died of his wounds.

Another explosive weapon that operatives often employed for assassinating high-value targets was the mine. This weapon was designed to be buried under, or placed upon, the ground and typically detonated when pressure was inadvertently placed upon it by the unsuspecting enemy. It came in either an anti-personnel or an anti-tank variant.

*Tactics Tip: Assassination with a Mine* (see opposite) recounts a famous example of operative assassination using such a device: the 1943 Byelorussian Partisan attack on the brutal Nazi Commissar for White Russia, Wilhelm Kube.

## Limpet Mines

The limpet mine was also a favoured weapon among maritime operatives. This was a magnetized naval mine that a diver could attach to the steel sides of the target vessel under the waterline. Having been delivered to the proximity of the target by a small motor vessel, submarine or midget submarine, the two-man team of divers would either canoe or swim to the enemy vessel. If operating in a

# Limpet Mine

**A favoured weapon employed principally by Allied secret operatives on maritime strikes was the limpet ine, a naval magnetic mine device. The weapon could be brought covertly to the approximate area of the target by a small motor vessel, a submarine or a midget submarine.**

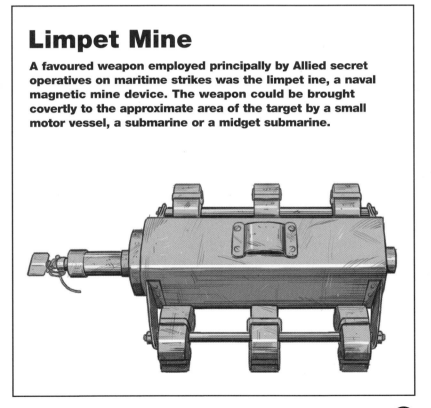

# Mission Profile:
# Assassination – Target Hitler

During 1944, SOE began actively planning Operation 'Foxley', the assassination of Adolf Hitler. To realize this aim, SOE began amassing all the bits of intelligence in Allied possession concerning the Berghof, Hitler's alpine residence in Berchtesgaden in southern Bavaria. This planning identified four possible means of assassinating Hitler: a long-range sniper strike; a bazooka attack; an IED attack (by throwing a suitcase full of explosive under his train); and, finally, poisoning the train's water supply.

The planning did not proceed beyond this stage, so the challenging questions of who might undertake such a mission, how they would reach the target area, how they would effect the assassination and how they might escape thereafter were never fully addressed. The viability of the plot, while theoretically possible, remained rather fanciful, particularly as it was dependent on getting accurate and precise warning of Hitler's movements sufficiently early for the plot to be initiated – a challenging requirement, given the secrecy under which senior Nazi leaders now operated.

Undeterred by these difficult practicalities, SOE also commenced planning a series of assassinations of key Nazi figures such as the Reichsführer-SS, Heinrich Himmler and the Propaganda Minister, Josef Goebbels; this planning actively considered the employment of chemical poisons and biological toxins.

canoe, one diver held himself (and thus the canoe) in position alongside the ship with a magnetic holdfast while the other would lower the limpet mine down through the water using a 2m (6ft 6in) rod and attach it to the vessel's hull.

Early British limpet mines contained 4kg (9lbs) of explosive. Successful attachment of the mine to the target vessel was the most challenging part of such missions; in response, SOE produced small numbers of the Welmine, a powered

1. Timing.

The readiest indication of Hitler's presence in the OBERSALZBERG is the big swastika flag which is flown on such occasions from the flagpole at the car park in front of he BERGHOF. Amongst other view-points this flag is visible from the SCHELLENBERG-UNTERAU road (Fig.1), the Café TOTTENHOFER (Fig.30), and the DOKTORBERG, both in Berchtesgaden.

Another indication is the presence in the neighbourhood of various Sonderzüge (special trains), viz. Hitler's at Schloss KLESSHEIM sidings (Fig61), Keitel's at BISCHOFSWIESEN, the Gästezug (visitors' train) at Berchtesgaden and Rippentrop's train at Salzburg (Fig.62).

A third clue to Hitler's presence at the OBER SALZBERG is provided by the clientele of the Wirthaus HOFSHAFFNER (Fig.30) in Berchtesgaden, a tavern much frequented in the evening by members of the SS Führerbegleitkommando when off duty.

(Extract from paper prepared for execution of Operation Foxley).

mine (effectively, a mini-torpedo) that came in magnetic, jettison-head and percussion variants.

**Poison**

Another method employed by operatives for assassination was poison. During 1944–45, for example (as described in *Mission Profile: Assassination – Target Hitler*), SOE planned the assassination of key Nazi leaders, including Hitler, Himmler and Goebbels, under the codenames Operation 'Foxley' and 'Little Foxley'.

# Attaching a Limpet Mine to a Ship

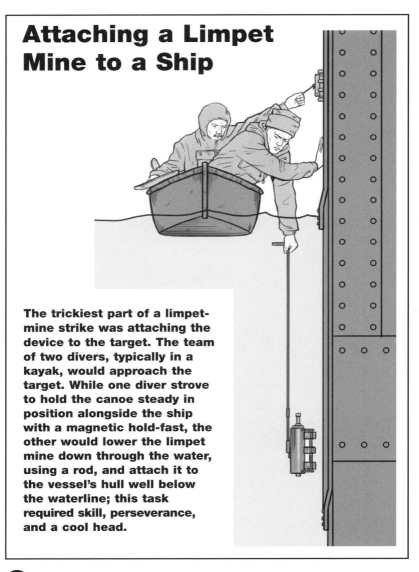

The trickiest part of a limpet-mine strike was attaching the device to the target. The team of two divers, typically in a kayak, would approach the target. While one diver strove to hold the canoe steady in position alongside the ship with a magnetic hold-fast, the other would lower the limpet mine down through the water, using a rod, and attach it to the vessel's hull well below the waterline; this task required skill, perseverance, and a cool head.

# Operation 'Jaywick'

One famous operative limpet mine attack was Operation 'Jaywick'. In September 1943, 14 Australian naval commandos and sailors from Special Operations Australia's Z Special Unit journeyed from Australia to Singapore harbour in a small Asian fishing vessel. With secrecy paramount, the operatives stained their skin with dye and ensured that they only threw overboard the remains of authentic local cuisine. Having reached the vicinity of harbour on the night of 24–25 September, the commandos paddled themselves 31 miles (50km) in two- and three-man Hohn Folbot collapsible kayaks to a cave on an island adjacent to the harbour. On the following night they quietly paddled themselves up to the sides of seven Japanese vessels docked in the harbour. They attached their limpet mines using delivery-rods and then paddled back to the cave. The ensuing explosions sank the seven vessels. To avoid the inevitable ensuing Japanese searches, the commandos lay low at the cave until 2 October, when they paddled back to their fishing boat, which took them successfully back to Australia.

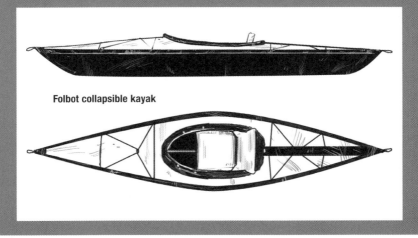

**Folbot collapsible kayak**

The planning included detailed discussion of the viability of mounting such assassinations using chemical poisons and biological toxins.

SOE planning identified four ways of poisoning a high-value target: ingestion via mouth; inhalation; injection; and absorption through the skin. Ingestion required the operative to poison the target's food or water. Inhalation was considered to be the most effective method, as Botulism (Agent W) was very effective via inhalation, while Anthrax (Agent N) was similarly lethal in even the tiniest doses (thus aiding concealment). An operative could expose either of these substances in the target's quarters or on his/her clothing. Injection could be very effective, but the challenge for the operative was to get sufficiently close to the target to administer it; SOE felt that needles hidden in fountain pens were likely to be detected by routine enemy searches. In addition, unless the victim was unconscious, they

# Nivea Cream

**In theory, secret operatives could contaminate with poisons or toxins many creams, gels, liquids or solids used on a daily basis by the enemy. In practice, the implementation of such plans was rare; Polish Resistance, however, did lace a jar of German Nivea Cream, like this one, with mustard gas.**

would instantly be aware of the attack, threatening the viability of the operative's escape. SOE's planners also believed that while poisoning by absorption through the skin was theoretically possible, it would be extremely difficult to achieve. The inside of the target's gloves, for example, might be contaminated with Agents N and W, but the garment would need to be worn for a long time to allow sufficient absorption to take place; in the meantime the garment might be discarded or lost.

SOE operatives undoubtedly took poisons with them to Nazi-occupied Europe; agents sent to Norway and Denmark in 1942, for example, carried half-inch Prussic Acid 'lethal tablets'. Operatives also had Cyanide 'suicide' tablets, often fitted into the end of the earpiece of a pair of glasses, or concealed within a coat or jacket button, for use in case of capture.

While SOE considered using such poisons to carry out assassinations, in reality it rarely happened; this method required the operative to get very close to the victim, and there were always other viable methods for achieving the mission. There is some circumstantial evidence that suggests that the British Type 73 anti-armour hand grenade used to kill Reinhard Heydrich may have been modified to contain Botulinum toxin; however, as there is little supporting evidence behind the documented strange

modification of the device, this argument has generally not received widespread acceptance.

Local Resistance operatives, however, did on occasion attempt assassination by poison. According to intercepted German messages dated February 1944, a Polish Resistance unit planted two tins of doctored Nivea face cream in a German camp. These aroused sufficient suspicion for the Germans to send them off for analysis; the cream was found to be impregnated with mustard gas. The Germans, meanwhile, also planned several assassinations using poison, as described in *Tactics Tip: German Poison Roulette* (see p226).

## Kidnapping

Another, admittedly rare, form of operative offensive action, other than assassination, was kidnapping. As this was significantly more challenging to achieve than assassination, and ultimately less of a permanent solution, it was only undertaken in exceptional circumstances.

One situation in which this might occur was when a particular enemy leader needed to be liquidated, but it was feared that assassination would lead to harsh reprisals against the local population, as occurred after the killing of Heydrich.

In early 1944, for example, two SOE operatives based in Cairo,

## Tactics Tip:
# German Poison Roulette

During early March 1945, the Allies captured one female and three male German operatives who had been inserted into northern France on 2 March by parachute from one of the only seven captured American B-17 bombers pressed into *Luftwaffe* service. Under interrogation, the agents revealed the poison weapons Germany had developed with which their agents were to assassinate Allied commanders. One such weapon was a tiny (1mm diameter) spherical pellet of an unspecified poison that was to be placed in cigarette trays; the heat of nearby lit cigarette ash vaporized the pellet, killing anyone nearby. The Germans also produced substantial quantities of chocolate laced with poison.

The final such weapon was a doctored glass tube of Bayer's aspirin tablets, which was to be employed in a parody of Russian roulette. Among the tube's 10 tablets were two that contained poison; identical to the others, the agent only knew which ones were poisoned by their position within the tube. The Germans intended that this weapon would be used by female agents against Allied officers travelling on trains. After offering the target a doctored cigarette that induced a headache, the agent was then supposed to offer the victim a tablet, while first taking an undoctored aspirin herself to allay the target's fears. The doctored aspirin, laced with an unknown poison, was said to induce death within 10 minutes of ingestion, allowing time for the agent to move to another carriage or leave the train at the next station.

Major Patrick Leigh Fermor and Captain William Stanley Moss, developed a plan to kidnap the German Military Governor of Crete, General Friedrich-Wilhelm Müller, who had a brutal reputation. By mounting a bloodless kidnap attributable solely to SOE operatives, Leigh Fermor hoped to prevent reprisals against the local populace.

On 4 February, the two British agents, plus two Cretan SOE

operatives, attempted to parachute into Crete, but bad weather prevented all but Leigh Fermor from doing so; after three further abortive parachute attempts, the remaining operatives arrived by motor launch on 4 April.

By then General Heinrich Kreipe had replaced Müller as governor, but the agents nevertheless decided to proceed with the mission. On the night of 26 April, the two British operatives, dressed as German military police corporals, stopped the General's car at a road block that they had established. Moss coshed the driver unconscious and then calmly drove the car, with Kreipe inside, for 90 minutes through no fewer than 22 German roadblocks before abandoning the car, leaving behind documents that incriminated British commandos.

Moving across country on foot, the operatives and Cretan aides evaded German search patrols. On the way they crossed Mount Ida, the mythical birthplace of the god Zeus; here, bizarrely, Kriepe and Fermor amiably discussed Horace's Ode to the mountain. The team eventually rendezvoused with a British motor launch on a beach near Rodakino and were transported to Egypt.

## Ambushes and Raids

In addition to sabotage and assassination, operatives located behind enemy lines also engaged the enemy by conducting ambushes and raids. In an ambush, a lone operative, or more commonly a small team, utilized surprise and concealment to attack a typically larger enemy force from a position of advantage. Although the difference could be a fine one, ambushes differed from assassinations in that they generally did not target a specific 'high-value' individual but rather sought to write-off whatever enemy personnel and equipment was present.

The key feature of the single 'point' ambush was that operatives initiated the attack at the time, location and method of their choosing. Well concealed behind hedges, bushes, trees, ditches or walls, or within houses that overlooked the ambush site, the operatives would wait for the unsuspecting targets to approach – typically along a road or track – and then initiate the ambush with withering fire.

### Raids

Although the distinction could sometimes be a fine one, a typical raid differed from an ambush in that the operatives attacked a fixed enemy location, generally an important target such as a key headquarters, a facility that deployed a potent new weapon, or a crucial industrial installation. The aim of the raid, just like the ambush, was to write-off enemy personnel and

# Sniper Targets

A secret operative sniper would carefully select his/her targets and the sequencing of his/her shots, to ensure mission success. The sniper might select the tyres of an enemy vehicle, to hinder enemy mobility, or aim to puncture fuel tanks.

**aiming to assassinate a nemy leader, he would wait r the right movement for a lear head shot.**

equipment, although some raids could aim to inflict sabotage.

While many raids were carried out by operatives working with local Resistance groups or Partisans, others were carried out by conventionally configured special forces such as Commandos and airborne forces; in a typical raid, the force involved was sizable, with anywhere between 10 and 200 personnel committed.

One famous raid occurred on 28 March 1942, when 265 British Commandos raided the port of St Nazaire in western France to destroy key dockyard installations. Another seminal example, as previously discussed in Chapter 5, 'Sabotage', was the two attempts by SOE-trained Norwegian operatives and Norwegian commandos to destroy the heavy-water facility at Vermork in Norway, which the Germans could have used as part of a nuclear weapons programme to make an atomic bomb.

### Ambushes

Operatives planning to carry out an ambush needed to consider five key elements in the technique of this type of mission: the ambush's objective, location, timing, and method, as well as the subsequent exfiltration. The objectives behind such ambush missions not only varied widely but also overlapped. Many such attacks aimed to harass and tie down enemy forces, while also sapping their physical and psychological strength. Other attacks aimed to write-off an important target such as a local commander or a potent new piece of equipment. Other ambushes aimed to inspire local Resistance forces into stepping-up their guerrilla warfare activities. One objective that all ambushes shared, however, was that they aimed to inflict significant losses on the enemy while minimizing own-side casualties.

**Location**
In selecting the best location for the ambush, operatives had to consider: the ease of covert approach to the selected location; which site maximized the impact of surprise and permitted them to exploit the terrain; and how easy it would be for them to extract afterwards. Operatives would carefully reconnoitre the known route of the enemy force, say a regular patrol or small convoy, and identify the best location to ambush

# Room Clearing

**An operative strike team aiming to clear a building would split into sub-teams and either enter rooms via doors or after blasting a hole in an adjoining wall; the emphasis would be on exploiting speed and the enemy's confusion to quickly kill or capture the defending forces.**

# Sniper Scope Types

**Sniper sights are either of a single post (left) or crosshairs (right) type. The tiniest variation in the angle that the sniper looks through the sight affects the fall of the shot. This diagram shows the relationship between changes in the angle of viewing and the landing of the round.**

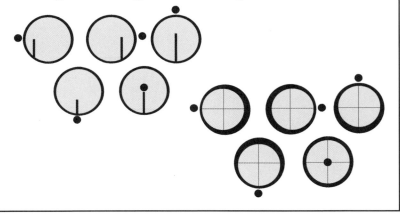

them; in addition, they would also get information from local Resistance groups or sympathizers. The spot selected had to enable the force to approach the target area without detection, so operatives preferred broken terrain with plenty of cover (trees, hedges, ditches) or covered approaches (hedge-lined tracks, for example) that avoided buildings or hamlets (where enemy personnel might be billeted among the local population), and which did not having regular enemy patrols or convoys

passing through. In terms of timing the approach, operatives might approach the target area well before the attack, to facilitate preliminary reconnaissance. If the ambush was to be staged in daylight hours, the operatives often approached the location the previous night under cover of darkness, and then remained concealed until the ambush was initiated. Another concern was which location best enabled them to exploit the ground to maximize the effect of surprise.

# Road Ambush

A meandering road offered good opportunities for an ambush. The attackers would attempt to destroy, or at least disable, the front and rear vehicles of the enemy column, trapping the rest. The attackers would then pour withering fire into the front, centre and rear of the enemy column.

# Mission Profile: Assassination – Target Heydrich

The war's most famous SOE assassination was that against *SS-Obergruppenführer* (General) Reinhard Heydrich in Prague on 27 May 1942. An infamous Nazi, Heydrich was Reich-Protector of Bohemia and Moravia, and in London the Czechoslovak government-in-exile had resolved to kill him. SOE trained nine Czechoslovak volunteers and on 28 December 1941 a Halifax bomber flew to Czechoslovakia, where they parachuted in.

One location on Heydrich's usual car journey was a prime place for an ambush; near a tram stop, his car had to slow down to negotiate a hairpin turn. On 27 May, two agents, Jozef Gabcík and Jan Kubis, waited at the spot: the former was armed with a Sten submachine gun, and the latter with an improvised bomb. A nearby accomplice, reading a newspaper, signalled a warning that the target was approaching. As the car slowed, Gabcík stepped forward, aimed and attempted to fire his Sten, but the weapon jammed. Heydrich's panicked driver did an emergency stop, while the general stood up and drew his pistol. Reacting quickly, Kubis threw his bomb; the ensuing explosion wounded Heydrich. The operatives then made good their escape by bicycle and opted to lie low in a Prague church crypt. Despite an

apparently successful operation, Heydrich died of an associated infection on 4 June 1942. The Germans discovered the operatives' hideout and on 18 June, during a four-hour assault, Kubis was killed while Gabcík committed suicide rather than be captured.

Believing (incorrectly) that locals from the villages of Lidice and Lezáky were involved in the plot, the Germans executed both villages' entire adult male populations, deported the remainder, and razed both settlements to the ground. In all, 5000 Czechs died in the German terror that followed Heydrich's assassination – a sobering brake on further Allied-sponsored assassinations.

# Using an SMG

At short-range (less than 20m/65ft), automatic fire ('spray and pray') from a sub-machine gun is the most effective method for maximizing the chances of a lethal kill.

At longer ranges (more than 45m/148ft), the more selective semi-automatic fire was more effective.

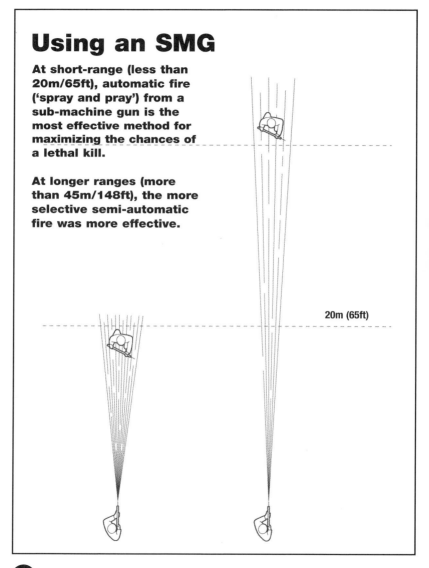

20m (65ft)

Operatives would select a location where the terrain rendered the target slow, exposed, overlooked and constrained in movement and reaction. If attacking a road convoy, operatives might select an area where the vehicles had to slow down, such as the hairpin bend selected in Heydrich's assassination. They might select an area where the convoy was exposed, for example when it went over a hump-backed bridge or an embankment and/or where it was overlooked, such as from the sides of a cutting or the upper story of a building. Finally, operatives needed to select an ambush site that allowed them to extract themselves easily and quickly after the mission had been carried out.

## Timing

The second key consideration for operatives planning an ambush was the timing of the strike. Operatives could mount ambushes in both daylight and in darkness. Daylight afforded the advantages of easier identification of the target, effective delivery of fire and better observation (and thus reaction) to enemy responses after being ambushed. However, ambushes during daylight also made it easier for the enemy to fight back and made it harder to evacuate the scene undetected after the attack. A night-time attack magnified the shock inflicted upon the enemy by a surprise ambush,

hindered the enemy's response to the attack, and facilitated a covert evacuation from the scene. That said, however, darkness brought additional confusion and chaos, making it harder to coordinate a successful ambush, and also brought with it an increased risk that friendly-fire casualties might occur amid all the confusion.

## Method

The third, and crucial, consideration was the method of the ambush; the tactics employed owed much to the situation's circumstances – what capabilities did the operatives possess, what were the target's vulnerabilities, and what advantages did the selected location have to offer? When attacking a road convoy, many routes offered ample opportunities for an ambush, most commonly when a sharp bend forced any convoy to slow; but when the route offered no such opportunities, the operatives would have to force the convoy to stop.

One way in which operatives could compel the lead vehicle to stop was by placing a tyre-bursting device. SOE employed the Caltrop, a small tetrahedron of three sharpened metal blades that could be strewn across a road, as well as a small explosive device in a container convincingly designed to resemble horse dung or a cow-pat. Alternatively, operatives could create a temporary barrier, such as by cratering the road with explosive, or by placing an apparently broken-down vehicle across it. But because these blocking methods had to be done some time before the target arrived, they ran the risk of compromising surprise. Alternatively, operatives could force a convoy's lead vehicle to stop by destroying or disabling it with small-arms fire or grenades, or by killing or incapacitating the crew. Operatives might place an anti-vehicle mine or other Improvised Explosive Device (IED) on the road to destroy the lead vehicle, or else they might string up wire between trees across a road to kill the motorcycle outrider who might be leading a convoy. Using mines to destroy the lead vehicle and so block the road was the method employed by SOE operative David Smiley and Albanian Resistance activists in the ambush initiated on 12 August 1943 at Kurtëîs in south-eastern Albania against a 23-vehicle

# Caltrops

**Calthrops (or Caltrops) were in essence a medieval weapon of metal spikes employed to hinder enemy horse-drawn movement along a route, although in modern times they were also employed to deny movement to an enemy wheeled vehicle, by puncturing its tyres.**

# PIAT

**The Projector, Infantry, Anti-tank was, from 1943 onwards, a standard British Army piece of equipment that occasionally saw use by operatives, Resistance activists or Commando forces behind enemy lines. It was the first British man-portable personal anti-armour device, and was highly effective at short range (typically, under 100m/328ft).**

German convoy. Such blocking tactics worked most effectively on narrow routes surrounded by embankments, hedges, trees, buildings, or ditches, where movement around the blocked vehicle was difficult or impossible.

As an alternative to blocking the lead vehicle, operatives often chose to initiate the ambush by destroying or disabling the lead vehicle by fire – using small-arms fire to wound or kill the driver, or to shooting out its tyres; using grenades, or by using, from 1943, the SOE Spigot mortar or, from 1944, the PIAT anti-tank launcher to disable it.

While the latter were used on occasion, because such weapons were large and cumbersome, operatives typically preferred to use grenades or IEDs.

### Killing Zones

In many ambushes, operatives simultaneously destroyed or disabled the convoy's front and rear vehicles, trapping the remainder in the middle of the ambusher's killing zones.

Once the convoy was stopped, some members of the ambush team would be in well-selected covered positions to bring accurate fire down on enemy personnel as they dismounted their vehicles and attempted to fire back.

If the ambush was initiated from one side of the road, it was logical for the surprised target personnel to disembark and seek cover on the adjacent side to fire back. Part of the ambush team may well have remained quiet up to this point, positioned on the opposite side to bring fire down on enemy personnel attempting to escape the fire of the rest of the ambush team.

To maximize fire-effect, SOE operatives working with the local Resistance often positioned themselves in an L-shaped ambush formation. Such positioning not only provided the attackers with the ability to strike the enemy from two sides simultaneously, but also produced excellent interlocking arcs of fire,

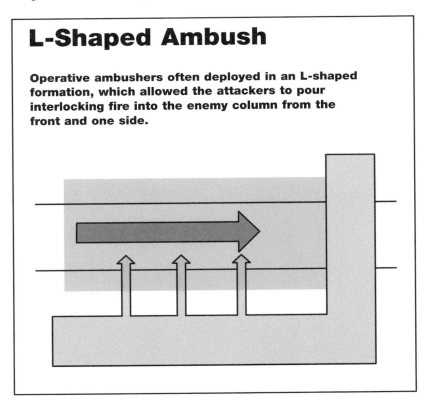

# L-Shaped Ambush

**Operative ambushers often deployed in an L-shaped formation, which allowed the attackers to pour interlocking fire into the enemy column from the front and one side.**

# V-Shaped Ambush

**Attackers also favoured deploying in a V-shaped formation. After waiting for the enemy column to move deep towards the apex of the V, all the attackers would simultaneously unleash fire from three sides, benefitting from murderous interlocking arcs of fire.**

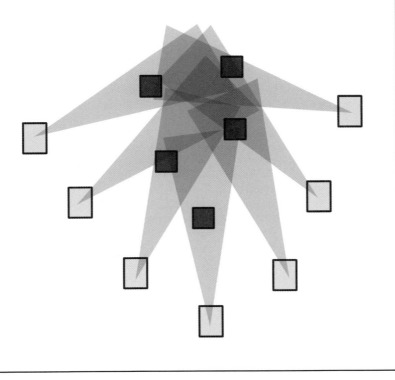

# Mission Profile:
# Ambush at Lus la Croix Haute

At 00:10 28 June 1944, the 15-man OSS Operational Group 'Justine' parachuted into south-eastern France to assist the local Resistance in their guerrilla war against the Germans. On 7 July, the team and 30 *Maquis* set up an ambush on a 100-yard U-shaped section of road in the hills near Lus la Croix Haute. The road's unusual shape, of course, enabled the operatives to pour fire simultaneously into the front, rear and centre of any approaching convoy. An unsuspecting German column approached, and the operatives rained fire down upon it, knocking out three vans and a truck.

The ambush inflicted heavy casualties on the enemy, killing 60 and wounding 25. Once the surviving German troops had managed to locate covered firing positions, however, they began to bring accurate small-arms fire on the ambushers.

Following the ambush's primary logic – only attack enemy weakness with the ambushers' strength from a position of advantage – at this point, the ambushers broke off the encounter before they suffered any significant casualties. Extricating at this point ensured that their strength could be used in future to inflict further casualties on the enemy in similarly executed ambushes.

maximizing the lethal effect of such a killing zone.

Another common Allied operative ambush formation was the V-shaped ambush. In this approach, the well-concealed operatives allowed the enemy column to advance close up to the apex of their V formation; and the ambushers would then simultaneously hit the hapless enemy with intense fire from three sides, again with the benefit of excellent interlocking arcs of fire. Other ambush tactics employed by Allied operatives included positioning some part of the ambush squad further away as a 'cut-off' – to cover with fire a track through or along which elements of the enemy might seek to retreat, often in disarray. Indeed, it was often in such 'cut-off' aspects of the ambush that the attackers achieved the greatest lethal effect again the enemy.

### Exfiltration

The final consideration for operatives selecting an ambush site was the exfiltration. Having conducted the ambush, the force needed to get away from the scene quickly, yet covertly, so as not to be detected or tracked. Ideally, the site's terrain ought to be conducive to the ambushers being able to extract at any moment, particularly if the enemy seemed to be gaining the upper hand in any fire-fight.

One ideal ambush location might have relatively good secondary tracks away from buildings along which the operatives could flee on bicycle; if operating with local Resistance forces, the ambushers might have available a farm truck carrying goods or hay, in which the operatives might be concealed. With all vehicles moving in the vicinity of the aftermath of an ambush likely to be searched, the operatives would need to be very well hidden, for example under the false floor of an open truck.

Operatives, of course, rarely identified a location that scored high marks in respect of all of these considerations, and during the planning and reconnaissance phases the team leader would have to make hard choices concerning the preferred location, trading off relative advantages or disadvantages in approach, fire-effect and ease of extraction. *Mission Profile: Ambush at Lus la Croix Haute* (opposite) describes how OSS operatives and French Resistance activists mounted one particular raid in south-eastern France, and the effect achieved.

### Area Ambushes

In addition to the operatives' 'point' ambush, described above, OSS and SOE agents operating in Nazi-occupied Europe also conducted area (baited trap) ambushes. This comprised a series of carefully planned interconnected ambushes; because this tactic required a significant force of at least 50 combatants, it was usually only carried out by those operatives working with established local Resistance groups.

The main ambush team would attack the target force, typically a convoy moving down the road, but permit some enemy personnel to escape and report the attack; meanwhile, several smaller ambush teams had established themselves at vantage points along the obvious routes toward the initial ambush; when enemy reinforcements moved

# Baited Trap Ambush

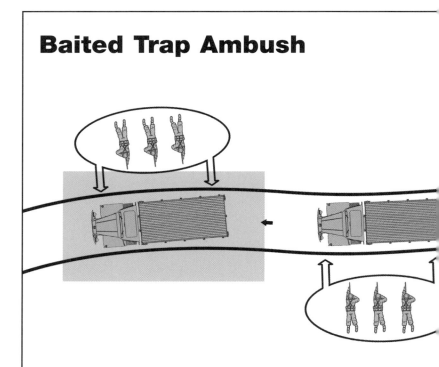

In a 'baited' ambush, the main body of attackers would ambush the main enemy column (here, seen on left), and then, when enemy relief columns (right) moved up to assist their stricken comrades, they would also be ambushed.

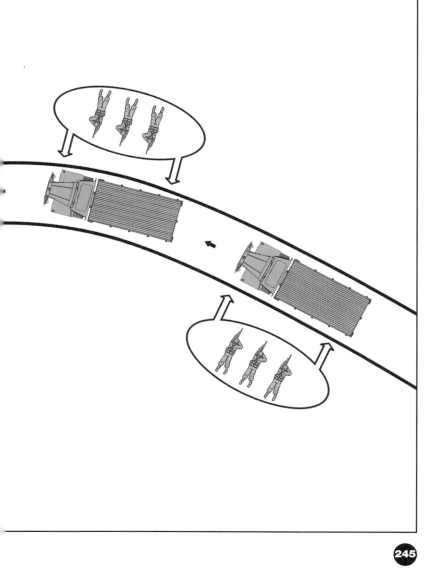

up to rescue the ambushed force, the ambush teams would subject them to withering fire.

These ancillary attackers could often be successful, for even though the enemy force was alert to the danger of attack, in their haste to rescue the ambushed main force, relief columns often took risks by not carrying out security measures, such as scouts and flank guards, that might otherwise slow their advance to the beleaguered main force.

## Guerrilla Warfare

The final type of operation in which operatives directly engaged the enemy was through conducting guerrilla warfare. This involved small groups of operatives, utilizing local knowledge and local support, repeatedly engaging the enemy over many months or years, in a long series of assassinations, ambushes, raids and sabotage missions. Allied special operatives conducted guerrilla warfare in two distinctive approaches. First, these operatives themselves directly executed guerrilla warfare against the enemy; secondly, these operatives trained, advised, organized, equipped, motivated or otherwise assisted local Resistance groups to conduct guerrilla warfare against the enemy.

### SAS operations

Some of the first instances of British operatives conducting guerrilla

# British Type B Mark II Radio Set

**A common suitcase-type communications device employed by SOE and OSS from 1942 onwards; each 'Jedburgh' team, for example, was equipped with one of these sets.**

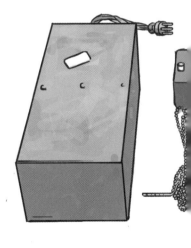

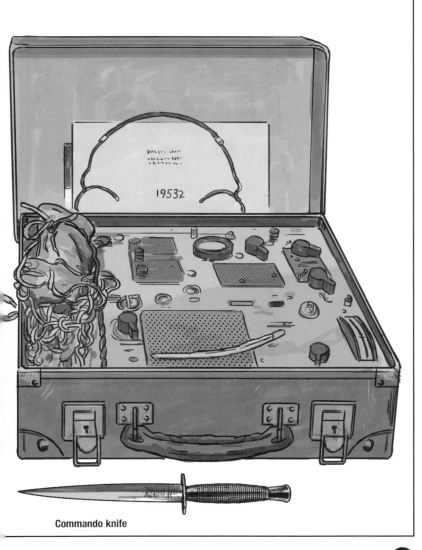

19532

Commando knife

warfare behind enemy lines occurred during the 1941–42 North African campaign. Under the cover of darkness, the vehicles of the Long Range Desert Group (LRDG) transported five-man SAS teams deep behind enemy lines. Using the stars to navigate, the SAS teams approached an enemy airfield. Silently digging under the perimeter wire, the operatives would crawl up to parked Axis aircraft or fuel containers and plant delayed-action incendiary bombs, before extracting themselves back to a pre-arranged timed rendezvous with LRDG vehicles. In December 1941 alone, such teams destroyed more than 70 Axis planes.

The direct waging of guerrilla warfare by Allied special operatives, however, was not confined to the early phase of the war. Indeed, in the months following the D-Day landings, the Allies inserted operatives behind enemy lines to conduct short-term guerrilla warfare to aid the forward momentum of nearby advancing friendly forces.

In Operation 'Amhurst', initiated on 7 April 1945, for example, some 50 15-strong teams from the 3rd and 4th (French) SAS Regiments dropped by parachute behind German lines in Holland. Their primary mission was to capture and hold key bridges and road junctions until relived by advancing Allied forces; simultaneously, they

were to block the arrival of German reinforcements and harass retreating enemy forces. Using the sorts of ambush and raid tactics discussed in detail above, these forces inflicted heavy casualties on the enemy. On dozens of occasions, the SAS teams lay undercover, adjacent to roads, ready to ambush German vehicles with their man-portable PIAT anti-tank launcher.

## Organizing Resistance Groups

The use of Allied operatives directly to conduct guerrilla warfare, however, remained less common than employing such personnel to organize, train, mentor, advise, assist, equip and support local Resistance groups to conduct guerrilla warfare. Perhaps the most famous example of Allied operatives training and supporting local Resistance forces were the 'Jedburgh' teams dropped mainly into French territory during the June–August 1944 Allied invasion of Nazi-occupied northern France and the ensuing Normandy campaign.

A three-man 'Jedburgh' team comprised a British SOE, an American OSS and a native-speaking operative (in most cases French BCRA, but also Belgian or Dutch). Each team had a commander, an executive officer and an NCO radio-operator, who worked the powerful Type B Mark II radio set, which had a transmit range of over 800km (500 miles). Typically, each 'Jed' carried

# Mission Profile:
# 'Jedburgh' Team 'Giles'

During the night of 8–9 July 1944, 'Jedburgh' Team 'Giles's' three operatives – American Captain Knox, French Captain Lebel and British wireless-operator Sergeant Tack – parachuted into the Finisterre region of south-western Brittany. Its mission was to organize the French Resistance in central Finisterre, reported to number some 3000 mostly unarmed and barely trained personnel. The Allies hoped that such guerrilla warfare would tie down German forces and delay the arrival of reinforcements at the front line in Normandy. The 'Jedburgh' missions thus contributed directly to the success of the Normandy campaign. The team rendezvoused with local Resistance leaders who took them to a well-concealed camp in a remote wood. After receiving by parachute drop the additional weapons that Knox had requested from London by radio, the Resistance initially gathered useful intelligence before conducting numerous ambushes of German forces moving east towards the Normandy front line. By 4 September, Team 'Giles' had returned to London, its mission complete.

the airborne version of the American 7.62mm (0.3in) M1A1 carbine, a 9mm (0.35in) semi-automatic pistol, and a British Fairbairn-Sykes Commando knife. During the second half of 1944, British Handley-page Halifax and American consolidated B-24 Liberator aircraft dropped 93 three-person 'Jedburgh' teams into France by parachute under the cover of darkness. In addition to training, mentoring and assisting local Resistance groups, the 'Jedburgh' teams' main role was to communicate with Britain using one-time cipher pads for their radios to organize the dropping by parachute of weapons and munitions for these local groups. The 'Jedburgh' operatives remained with local Resistance groups for months until the Allied advance from Normandy reached the area that they were working in. Between them, local Resistance groups aided by 'Jedburgh' teams carried out thousands of ambushes, raids, acts

# Chin Jab

**Method for delivering an open-palm chin jab:**

1. **With hand open and fingers spread, jab base of palm as hard as possible into enemy's chin, violently throwing his head back.**
2. **Instantly thereafter, drive fingers into the enemy's eyes.**
3. **Exploit fleeting opportunity to inflict a lethal blow.**

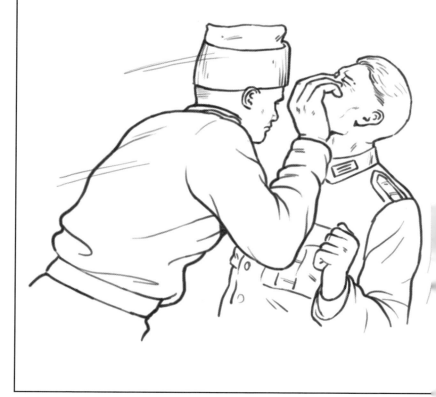

**Open palm**

of sabotage, and other guerrilla warfare-related activities, significantly assisting the Allied liberation of France. *Mission Profile: 'Jedburgh' Team 'Giles'* (p249) recounts the actions of one particular team.

## Close-Combat Skills

An operative tactic that might also have been employed in any assassination, ambush, raid or guerrilla warfare mission was the art of unarmed combat and silent killing. Unarmed combat involved stunning or (ideally) killing enemy personnel using only the human body, whereas silent killing involved the use of a knife, dagger or garrotte. This was a crucial capability for operatives to possess that could be employed in a number of ways.

In a raid on a compound, for instance, one operative could silently kill a sentry, permitting the rest of the team to enter the facility and simultaneously strike at the remaining guard positions with their small arms. In an assassination, where silence was crucial, for example when the victim could be approached while asleep, and where no suppressed firearms were available, an operative could take out the target with a commando knife.

Finally, as we shall see in the next chapter, in the worst case scenario, if an operative was captured, these skills would be essential element in any escape bid.

## Unarmed Combat

All operatives received training in unarmed combat and silent killing. Techniques of unarmed combat were based on the principle of using the human body to deliver the maximum shock effect on the opponent's weaknesses by utilizing surprise, speed and precisely delivered force. These skills could be used offensively and defensively. The SOE syllabus divided these unarmed combat skills into five sections: blows, hold releases, group fighting, knife combat, and special techniques such as killing sentries.

The 'blows' phase first taught operatives to make swift, sharp blows with the outer edge of the hand, aimed at the back of the opponent's neck, or face from nose to throat, or to the kidneys. This phase then went on to train them in other effective techniques such as the open-hand chin jab, knee jab to the opponent's groin, head-butt, elbow jab and the finger-tip jab to the enemy's eyes or throat.

The course's next phase taught operatives that, if their opponent had got them in a hold, they could break this with a release move such as a strangle release or a bear-hug release; alternatively, agents were taught to break holds by going onto the attack with a simultaneous knee-jerk to the groin and finger-jab to the eyes. The third phase trained operatives that, when facing several opponents, they had to keep continually moving, and use swift kicks to the opponents'

knees or feet to temporarily hinder the assailants so that the operative could attempt to escape at the earliest opportunity.

### Silent killing

The course's next phase taught operatives how to use the knife in either hand for stabbing into the opponent's abdomen, as well as slashing across the enemy's face or through his/her hamstring at the back of the knee.

The final phase taught special techniques, particularly killing sentries. Operatives were trained to attack sentries from the rear, chopping with the left hand into the enemy's neck, then instantly sliding the hand up to cover the mouth and nose to prevent them raising the alarm; simultaneously, the right hand thrust the knife deep into the kidneys as the left hand pulled the sentry down and backwards.

The course also taught unarmed operatives to kill sentries in the following fashion. Attacking from the rear, the agent smashed his/her right forearm onto the opponent's neck to stun him and then got the enemy in a head hold, forcing the sentry down to the operative's thigh. Then, the operative would suddenly sit down, while pulling the enemy's head up and twisting it, to break his neck. Alternatively, operatives were trained to implement the 'spinal dislocator', namely to break an opponent's back. Approaching from the rear, the operative placed his left hand under the sentry's chin and viciously pulled the head right back until it was under his/her right arm-pit. The agent then dropped his left wrist down onto the enemy's left shoulder while passing his/her right arm across the back of the sentry's head. The operative next gripped from above his/her left wrist with the right hand; a quick snap up and backwards would then break the sentry's spine.

The last periods of instruction taught operatives how to overpower a guard pointing a pistol, how to parry an enemy blow, and how to make various throws. At some point in many operative ambushes or raids, these skills were called upon. This training, as we have seen, enabled female operative 'Coco' to evade capture after being surprised

by a German soldier while laying explosives at a French railway signal box in France during June 1941.

In order to carry out successful assassinations, ambushes, raids and guerrilla warfare, therefore, operatives had to employ the full range of specialist weapons and equipment available to them. They also had to employ all their specialist skills and training in navigation, living-off-the-land, concealment, cross-country movement, and armed and unarmed combat in order to execute the given mission. Having accomplished the objective, the operatives' next task, as Chapter 7 recounts, was to escape from the immediate scene, avoid enemy attempts to capture them, and then and be extracted from behind enemy lines back to friendly territory, or at least to neutral territory, from where they might be able to make it back to home.

# Commando Knife

**The famous Fairbairn-Sykes fighting (or 'commando') knife was a sharply pointed, acutely tapered, double-edged poignard with a foil grip. It was employed from 1941 by British Commandos and the SAS, as well as by both SOE and OSS operatives.**

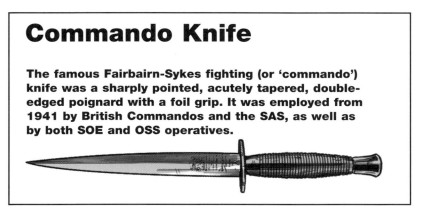

# Strangle Release

1. **Seize the underneath of your opponent's right elbow with your left hand, thumb to the right.**
2. **Using your right hand, reach over both your opponent's arms and seize his wrist.**
3. **Using your right forearm, apply downward pressure to your opponent's left arm; simultaneously, using a circular upward motion of your left hand, force his elbow inwards towards your right. This will break the stranglehold and imbalance him.**
4. **Gripping firmly with both hands, turn rapidly rightwards by bringing your right leg to your right rear, extending your opponent's right arm.**
5. **Mount a hand-edge blow on your opponent's exposed elbow.**

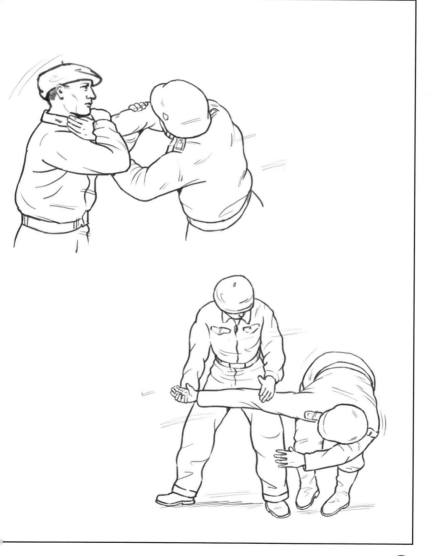

# Knee Jab

1. As shown left, drive knee as hard as possible up into your opponent's groin, while using your right hand to grasp his left shoulder to pull his torso downwards.
2. Exploit with head butt, or right-handed eye-gouge.

Alternatively, initiate a chin jab. As the enemy reels back from this blow, drive your knee up into his groin.

# Bear Hug Release

1. If possible, bite your opponent's right ear to make him bed forward.
2. Grab your opponent's testicles with your right hand.
3. Using your left forearm, reach over your opponent's right arm.
4. Using your left arm, apply pressure to your opponent's right arm, breaking the bear-hold and forcing his head downwards and towards your right.
5. Smash your opponent's face with your right knee and administer an edge of hand blow to his neck with your right hand.

# Attacking a Sentry

1. Silently approach sentry from rear.
2. Strike the enemy across the throat with the inner edge of your left hand.
3. Instantly slide hand up to cover sentry's mouth and nose.
4. Simultaneously, use your right hand to thrust knife deep into the sentry's kidneys, while left hand pulls sentry downwards and backwards.

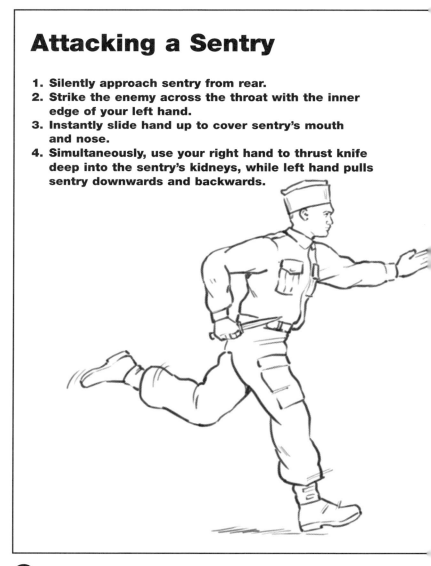

**5.** Once you have knifed the sentry, let go and bring your right hand up to cover enemy's mouth while using your left hand to pull sentry downwards and backwards.

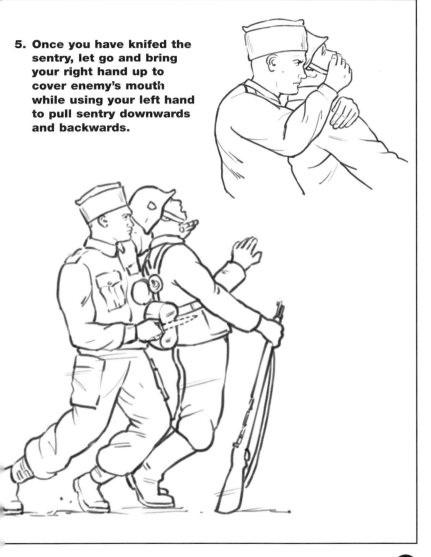

**A**fter completing their mission, whether an act of sabotage, an assassination, a raid or fostering guerrilla war, operatives then needed to extract themselves from enemy-controlled territory back to home. Of the 418 SOE agents inserted into Axis-controlled Europe, some 300 were extracted, as were 120 Resistance operatives. Extraction consisted of two distinct phases.

First, operatives needed to escape from the immediate scene of the mission and lie low in a safe house or some other secret location. Once this had been accomplished, operatives could then organize their extraction from behind enemy lines. From the perspective of SOE, successful extraction was crucial from the humanitarian motive of preserving its courageous human assets from enemy capture (which invariably led to privation, torture and often execution). Its operatives, moreover, were precious human assets in whom it had invested extensive training and who possessed specialized skills. These assets had to be preserved so that they could undertake future missions and train others to do the

. . . . . . . . . . . . . . . . . . . . . . . . . . . . . .

**Extraction – whether from the secne of an operation or escape from an occupied country – took many forms and required great skill and organization to be successful.**

# 7

**Once secret operatives had completed their mission, there were a number of ways they could escape.**

# Extraction

# Covering Your Tracks

**To avoid the enemy detecting and following their trail, operatives were trained to obliterate the evidence, as seen here, using foliage to swish away any telltale footmarks.**

same. Dozens of agents were inserted into and extracted from enemy lines on several occasions; Pierre Brossolette ('Brumaire'), for example, came out of France on three occasions and went back in three times.

These operatives also possessed detailed knowledge concerning their organizations, intelligence that the enemy was desperate to acquire. If captured alive, it was reasonable to assume that even with incredible fortitude, many operatives would eventually succumb to enemy torture and reveal at least some of what they knew. Operatives were thus issued with the means to commit suicide, in most cases a cyanide tablet that needed to be bitten or chewed to be activated.

In some instances, agents faced with imminent capture decided to commit suicide to escape it. When his hiding place in a Prague church crypt was stormed by German troops, for example, Jan Kubis, one of SS-General Heydrich's assassins, committed suicide rather than be captured alive. Similarly, after 'Brumaire' was captured he was taken to the German Security Police Headquarters at 84 Avenue Foch in Paris in March 1944 and tortured. Regaining consciousness in an unguarded garret attic, he jumped to his death from a fifth-floor window in what was probably a suicide attempt.

## Escape from the Immediate Scene

Once operatives had executed their mission, their first task was to get away from the scene. Many of them preferred to extricate themselves on foot. This method had the obvious disadvantage of being slow, and thus perhaps made it likelier that the operative might get caught up in the immediate enemy hue and cry that would inevitably

arise. That said, simply walking away brought two main advantages: it provided considerable flexibility and helped preserve stealth. By simply walking calmly, a well-trained operative possessing iron nerves, good local knowledge, authentic-looking documents, appropriate language skills and a convincing cover story, for example, might be able to bluff his/her way through an enemy checkpoint as an innocent local. There is nothing more innocuous than a civilian casually walking in an unhurried fashion down a street while a panicked enemy rushes around the area looking for a likely assailant, namely someone nervously rushing down a street, keeping to the shadows or racing off in a vehicle.

Some British SOE operatives, such as Major Patrick Leigh Fermor and Captain William Stanley Moss, clearly possessed the amazing degree of imperturbability and bravado required to pull off such bluffs. When kidnapping General Kreipe on Crete, Moss – dressed in German uniform – calmly drove the General's car for 90 minutes through 22 enemy checkpoints, while all the time his accomplice, Leigh Fermor, also in German uniform, held their victim at gunpoint in the back. Operatives escaping on foot could walk or crawl through various types of difficult terrain, such as hills, mountains, woods, forests and

# Bicycle Power

**Bicycles proved a useful way for operatives to move around without standing out or drawing attention to themselves. Many operatives preferred to escape from the scene using an innocuous local French civilian bicycle, such as the one depicted here, so as to blend into the background.**

marshes – terrain that the enemy might not expect them to attempt to cross and thus not search, at least not initially. By walking through remote and difficult mountainous terrain in Crete, Leigh Fermor, Moss, their Cretan aides and the kidnapped Kreipe made only slow progress, but they avoided all of the many dozens of enemy checkpoints that had been set up along all secondary roads and some minor tracks. In snow-covered theatres, such as Norway, cross-country movement on skis was the operatives' favoured form of extraction.

### Bicycles and Motorcycles

On other missions, operatives preferred to extricate themselves from the scene using a locally procured bicycle. This mode of escape was obviously quicker than walking but slower than using a motor vehicle. Yet utilizing a bicycle

also offered some flexibility, as it could be ridden over fields, along narrow tracks and through orchards, as well as along roads and tracks. Bicycles could also be ridden along alleys that were too narrow for pursuing vehicles to follow. On 7 December 1943 this facility enabled the cycling Danish operative Jens Lillelund to shake off the Gestapo officers pursuing him in their Opel car down Copenhagen's streets by

dashing down a side alley; his comrade Svend Otto Nielsen ('John') cycled down another street that did not afford this form of escape; forced to fight it out with his Welrod silenced pistol, 'John' was wounded seven times and taken prisoner. Denied medical care, the Gestapo tortured 'John' for weeks before executing him in April 1944.

An operative cycling along a minor dirt road, moreover, could quickly leap off his/her bike and drag it into the cover afforded by a roadside ditch or culvert, for example, when he/she observed approaching enemy vehicles. Bicycles were also extremely quiet, and cycling during night-time, while challenging in terms of navigation and the avoidance of obstacles, maximized the operative's secrecy. Moreover, a 'civilian' calmly cycling along in daylight did not

necessarily attract undue attention, a vital attribute for the operative's *modus operandi* (see *Tactics Tip: Innocuous and Unassuming*, opposite). After mounting the assassination strike against SS-General Heydrich, Kubis and Gabcík simply cycled away from the scene, abandoned his bike and sought shelter in an accomplice's house.

# The Welbike

**Despite being specially designed for SOE operatives, it was subsequently felt that the Welbike lacked the necessary stealth to be much use as a method for agents to escape from the scene of a mission.**

# Tactics Tip:
# Innocuous and Unassuming

The general public invariably assume that the 'ideal' special operative was a James Bond-style individual – charismatic, audacious and confident. Yet during the course of the war, SOE discovered that some of their most effective agents were those with an unassuming physicality and an innocuous persona. The apparently innocuous nature of the bicycle made it an attractive mode of escape for this unassuming sort of agent. In France, when a Gestapo squad arrived to search the vicinity of the house in which operative Roger Landes ('Aristide') had been transmitting from his radio, he calmly wheeled his bicycle through the German cordon. His unassuming physicality – he was just five foot four, slim built and often described as looking like a bank manager – worked in his favour, for when Landes accidently knocked off his bike-rack the suitcase containing the radio the Germans were searching for, a German soldier helped him pick it up. Once through the cordon, Landes nonchalantly cycled away as if without a care in the world.

Another possible means of escaping the scene was on a motorcycle. Such vehicles offered several main advantages: they were much quicker and possessed greater off-road capability than bicycles; and they could also be ridden along railway lines, a feat difficult to achieve with a bicycle. But the crucial disadvantage of motorcycles was that they were very noisy and so likely be noticed passing through the countryside. Despite this drawback, the British nevertheless developed the Welbike as a specialist portable folding motorcycle for use by SOE operatives (see *The Welbike,* opposite). During its field trials, however, the Welbike proved far too noisy, produced too much smoke, and performed inadequately off-road, so was not of much value to agents; consequently, most Welbikes were issued to British airborne forces. SOE also developed the Weasel, a collapsible motorized ski-sledge, for use in snowbound theatres like Norway.

## Equipment Profile:
# The Welbike

During 1942, the British developed the Welbike, a specially designed folding portable single-seat motorcycle for use by operatives. In total, over 3600 Welbikes were produced, although very few were actually taken to enemy-held Europe by SOE agents; it was too noisy and produced too many fumes for escaping operatives to preserve much secrecy. The Welbike was powered by a 98cc Corgi petrol engine and weighed just 32kg (70lbs). It was easy to assemble and disassemble, and when dismantled the entire vehicle fitted inside a standard British parachute airdrop container. It had a range of 145km (90 miles) and a maximum road speed of over 64km/h (40mph). While rarely used by the operatives for whom it was designed, it performed sterling service with the Allied airborne forces that fought in Nazi-occupied Europe.

# Blending In – Improvised Transport

### Other Vehicles

In other missions, operatives preferred to use a horsedrawn or motor vehicle as the quickest way of getting away from the scene.

**Operatives sometimes escaped the scene by hiding in an innocuous local farm-vehicle, sometimes, as seen here, under the hay on a horse-drawn hay wagon.**

This provided almost no degree of stealth, the operatives hoping that sheer speed would get them away from the area before any cordons could be established. However, any road travel brought the risk of an encounter with an enemy checkpoint or a military convoy, and so was a high-risk strategy. Using enemy vehicles might outwardly ward off

# MV Krait

**Australian operatives in disguise as local fishermen used the Asian fishing steamer *MV Krait* to transport themselves to the vicinity of Singapore harbour; from here, they used collapsible kayaks to attach limpet mines to the sides of Japanese shipping at anchor in the harbour. The same boat was then used to escape the scene and head back to Australia.**

casually scrutiny, but of course it invited local enemy personnel to enter into conversations with the fleeing operatives. But the latter ruse could work. As we have seen, Leigh Fermor and Moss, dressed in German uniform, used the cover of travelling in General Kreipe's official car to get themselves through 22 German roadblocks; what aided them here, of course, was that the enemy had yet to discover that the operative's mission to kidnap the general had already been executed.

To benefit from the speed of such vehicles, but without compromising secrecy, SOE and OSS agents received training in how to hide effectively in hay wagons or trucks carrying potatoes or other root vegetables. To the enemy, of course, a hay wagon was an obvious place to hide an operative or their weapons. On the stormy night of 30 August 1944, for example, the three-man OSS 'Jedburgh' team 'Augustus' were travelling at night disguised as locals with authentic papers in

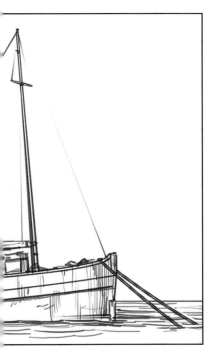

With good documents and language skills, a decent cover story, iron nerves and luck, an operative might get through such encounters. When Forest Yeo-Thomas ('White Rabbit') was travelling by train to Paris, he found himself engaged in light conversation with the man opposite him – the Lyon Gestapo Chief SS-Captain Klaus Barbie; keeping his nerve, Yeo-Thomas managed to escape this nerve-wracking encounter with his clandestine identity intact.

## Hiding Out

In numerous other missions, however, operatives instead opted to hide out in a nearby secure location, and wait for the inevitable enemy hullabaloo to die down before attempting to escape, rather than immediately trying to get distance between them and the scene. After all, the latter was what the enemy expected them to do. In late September 1942, for example, after Australian operatives had executed a successful limpet-mine attack that sank seven Japanese vessels in Singapore Harbour, the agents initially merely kayaked back to their nearby hiding place in a cave on a local island; only after seven days in hiding did the operatives paddle their folding kayaks the 50km (31 miles) back to MV *Krait*, the inconspicuous Asian fishing steamer that had brought them to Singapore. The option of

a horse-drawn cart that carried hay, under which they had hidden their weapons and radio. Caught by a German military checkpoint, the enemy discovered the weapons and summarily executed the agents. Other operatives instead opted to escape from the scene using public transport, notably trains, hoping to blend into the mass of ordinary civilians going about their daily business.

Trains, however, brought the prospect of encountering frequent searches of papers and questioning.

# Welman Midget

**SOE had designed a
small, one-man midget
submarine as depicted
here; as with other
SOE special creations,
such as the Welbike
and the Welrod, its
designation started
with the prefix 'Wel'.**

lying low *in situ*, however, did not
always turn out to be a successful
strategy. Kubis and Gabcík, for
example, the two SOE-trained
operatives who assassinated Heydrich,
decided to lie low until the hubbub had
died down, hiding in a Prague church
crypt. Unfortunately, their hiding place
was either betrayed or discovered by
the Germans and on 18 June, after 22
days in hiding, German forces stormed
the crypt and both agents died in the
ensuing battle.

### Escape by Water
In maritime target zones, or land-
based ones with considerable bodies
of water, operatives could swim

away from the scene. Swimming in
a generally land-based milieu had
several advantages over escape by
other means. At night, a swimmer
would be very hard to spot, and
with relatively little noise made, could
conserve secrecy and throw enemy
tracker-dogs off the scent they were
following. But swimming had its
drawbacks: it was slow and tiring; the
operative could carry little equipment,
was continually vulnerable to enemy
fire, yet unable to fire back; and
unless a change of clothing had
been taken in waterproof carriers,
the agent's subsequent endurance
would be impaired by cold; and an
individual soaked to the skin was

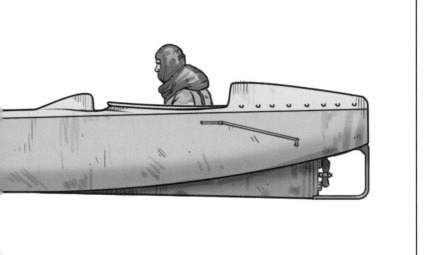

also extremely conspicuous.

So while rarely employed by operatives, in certain circumstances escape by swimming might be the only viable means of escape. After the Germans attempted to arrest operative Harry Rée ('César'), the wounded operative evaded his pursuers by swimming across a river and crawling 6.4km (4 miles) through a forest. With maritime targets such as enemy shipping, of course, the operatives invariably fled the scene using the method of approach. This could be by operatives silently paddling a canoe, collapsible kayak or raft; employing frogman diving gear, possibly when using the

'Sleeping Beauty' submersible canoe; utilizing their long-distance swimming skills; or being whisked away by a midget submarine (like the one-man Welman), a sailing vessel or a small motor boat.

## Extraction

Once well away from the scene of the mission, and hidden in a safe location, operatives could turn their thoughts to organizing how they would be extracted from behind enemy lines and safely returned to friendly territory. The process of extraction involved essentially the same techniques and skills described in Chapter 1. At this point, operatives

# German Radio-Intelligence Techniques

**The modus operandi of a German wireless interception company. The secret operative radio operator could be detected by short-range German wireless interception direction-finding devices (black arrows) or long-range devices (grey arrows).**

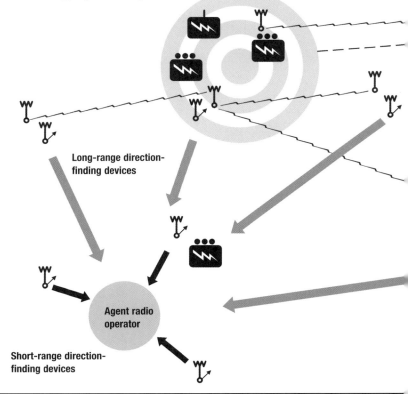

Long-range direction-finding devices

Agent radio operator

Short-range direction-finding devices

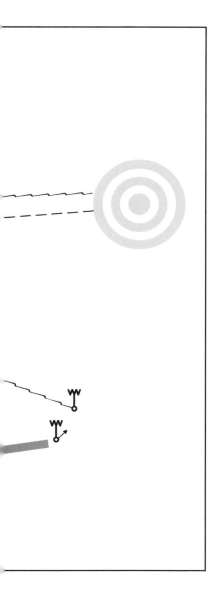

or their local Resistance friends communicated with Britain on a clandestine radio set. As we have seen in a previous chapter, SOE often replied to these messages by broadcasting seemingly innocuous announcements on the BBC, which many Resistance members secretly listened to; messages that carried a specific meaning to a particular group of listeners.

On the moonless night of 29–30 January 1944, for example, the BBC broadcast the message, 'Bonjour tout le monde à la Maison d'Alphonse'. This told the Dumais-laBrosse SOE group hiding in a remote farmhouse (known only to them as Alphonse's House) near Plouha in Brittany that the planned extraction by motorboat was under way. The extractees – two SOE agents and 16 escaped prisoners – set off on a silent march to the beach, where three dinghies arrived and took them to the waiting vessel.

Operatives making contact with London by clandestine radio, however, ran the risk of being detected by enemy counter-intelligence radio-transmission interception assets. Several SOE agents, including Yolande Beekman ('Mariette'), were captured by the Germans due, at least in part, to the enemy's identification of the rough location of the operatives' radios, while as is recounted in *Tactics Tip: Innocuous and Unassuming* (p269),

# Marking a Landing Zone

**If a 'reception committee' was expecting a relatively rare daylight landing, they might remove the topsoil to form an 'X' to indicate the correct landing spot, or perhaps make an 'X' in a crop field.**

the operative 'Aristide' just managed to escape capture in similar circumstances.

### By Air

Once contact had been made, London would typically dispatch a plane to extract the operatives from enemy territory. For such missions the British relied principally on one small light aircraft, the Westland Lysander Mk.IIIA(SD), as this aircraft

could be landed easily and quickly on a confined grass strip, and take off again quickly, bringing up to three operatives to safety. For extractions requiring greater lift capacity or range, the British employed the Lockheed Hudson from the RAF's 161 Squadron. This had an operational range of 1287km (800 miles), 322km (200 miles) more than the Lysander, and could carry up to 10 passengers; predictably, however, it needed a landing strip twice as long as that of the Lysander. On 24 July 1943, for example, a Hudson landed at a remote strip neat Saint Vulbas, north-east of Lyons in central-eastern France and transported eight French BCRA operatives back to England. The American OSS and on occasion the SOE for Balkan extraction missions also employed the Douglas C-47 Dakota.

For the operatives involved, though,what did a successful aerial extraction mission involve? Once radio communication had arranged the time and venue of the landing on some moonlit night, the operatives would prepare the landing strip. Once the landing strip was ready, the operatives would mark the site

for the incoming aircraft. Operatives and their assistants would place three such illuminations in a line, spaced at 100m (328ft) intervals, to mark out the left or right-hand side of the strip; to complete the 'flare path', a final illumination would be off-set to one side at the far end (thus forming an inverted 'L' shape) to indicate the width of the landing strip. Many 'reception committees' also signalled the agreed confirmation letter in Morse code to confirm that the illuminations were not an enemy trap, and/or communicated with the pilot using the S-Phone, as described in Chapter 1.

All these methods of illumination, however, worked on the basis

# Douglas DC-3 Dakota

**The US-designed Dakota transport aircraft was a common asset used for inserting operatives or their supplies by parachute behind enemy lines. The American OSS also employed the Dakota for extraction missions in the Balkans.**

that the SD-Lysander's sole crew member, the pilot, could navigate his plane at night to the general location of the landing strip using dead reckoning corrected by use of a wind triangle. All this was demanding on a long night journey, when the Lysander pilot was also doing the job of a navigator would normally do. To obtain real accuracy in navigation, however, the pilot had to correct these dead-reckoning calculations using visual recognition of distinctive geographical features (particularly lighthouses or canals/rivers that reflected the moonlight). Consequently, poor or deteriorating weather led the Allies to postpone many dozens of planned extraction flights, while dozens more also had to be abandoned in mid-flight.

The many Lysander flights that did make it successfully to the rendezvous, and spotted the illumination devices that marked the landing strip, still had to surmount the challenge of landing their aircraft on a rough and confined grass strip

# Wind Triangle

**A wind triangle, used to increase the accuracy of a pilot's dead reckoning, depicts three vectors: air vector (the aircraft's movement through the air, based on its air speed and heading); wind vector (the motion of the air over the ground based upon wind speed and wind direction); and the ground vector (the aircraft's movement over the ground, thus giving the aircraft's actual position, based on ground track and ground speed).**

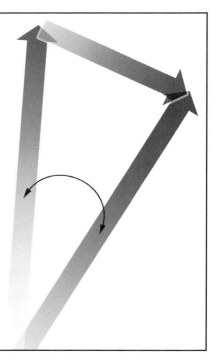

# Lysander Ladder

**The Lysander Mk.IIIA (SD) aircraft had a special ladder fitted to the port side of the aircraft's fuselage to enable operatives being inserted to get out of the rear cockpit quickly, and for agents being extracted swiftly to get up into the same cockpit.**

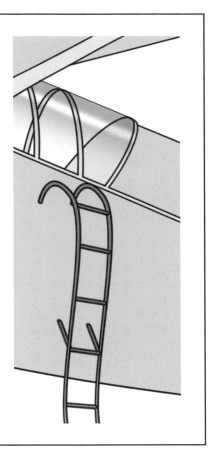

without crashing. During the war, four Lysanders crashed on landing: when Squadron-Leader Guy Lockhart landed his Lysander on a strip identified by flares near Mâcon in August 1942, the aircraft ploughed into a ditch and had to be destroyed;

John Mott's Lysander got bogged down on landing in 1942 and he was subsequently arrested by the Germans. Once the aircraft had landed, the operatives needed to climb up the ladder and into the plane's second cockpit as quickly as possible, to permit a swift take-off. Even when the operatives had embarked successfully, the mission still had to run a gauntlet of risks. The Lysander might crash on or shortly after take-off, be hit by enemy anti-aircraft fire, crash mid-flight due to mechanical failure, run out of fuel or crash on landing. During the war, seven Lysanders were lost on this return leg of the mission. In the early hours of 17 December 1943, for example, a Lysander ran short of fuel on returning from an operative extraction flight and crashed in foggy conditions just short of the runway at RAF Tangmere near Chichester; the pilot was killed and the two French operatives on board were badly injured. Within an hour of this crash, another Lysander returning from a similar mission crashed into a hillside near Ford Airfield outside Bognor Regis in Sussex while attempting to land.

## By Sea

SOE also extracted a proportion of its agents from enemy-held territory by sea, particularly from the coastal areas of north-west Europe, Norway, Denmark, the Mediterranean and in the Far East, where the geography favoured such methods. Night-time naval operative extraction had one main advantage over aerial extraction – it could take place on nights with little or indeed no moonlight when aerial extraction was impossible. The preferred Royal Navy vessels

# Morse Code

**Many 'reception committees' used torches to make the agreed 'Morse' code letter to verify themselves and to mark the place where the incoming aircraft was to land. Morse code consisted of short and long flashes (dots and dashes).**

employed for such missions were fast small craft, such as MTBs and MGBs. Such maritime operative insertion/extraction missions also involved surmounting a host of challenges – this method was just as risk laden as aerial extraction. Maritime extraction was also equally dependent on weather conditions

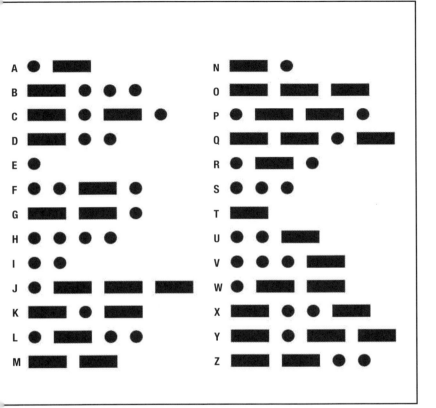

and the associated sea state and visibility, both of which were more likely to change during the vessel's longer journey, in comparison with aerial extraction.

The extraction vessel had to journey successfully to the vicinity of the agreed rendezvous, invariably a remote beach or cove on a dark moonless night while avoiding submerged rocks that had wrecked many previous unwary mariners. Once at the rendezvous, the operatives' 'reception committee' waiting on the shore would signal the pre-arranged letter by Morse code from a powerful lamp, to confirm not just the location but

# Flare Pistol

**Operatives and Resistance activists usually used torches, lamps or fires to mark out the grass airstrip on which the Lysander was to land. Occasionally, however, agents sometimes fired a flare pistol, such as this one.**

the identity of the signallers; in some cases, the committee would also fire a pistol flare. Having verified the identity of the signallers, and thus the correct location, the extraction vessel would cast off the four Warrington-Smyth SN-1 4.3m (14ft) wooden surf boats carried on its decks (or occasionally towed behind it). These surf boats were designed to be stable even in rough seas. Three specially trained men from the vessel's crew – a coxswain and two seamen – would silently row to shore. On occasion, the extraction craft alternatively used dinghies rather than surf boats, but they were a poor substitute, because in rough seas they turned over easily.

Once the surf boats or dinghies had reached the shore, the next challenge became successful and speedy disembarkation and embarkation of operatives, ideally within the five-minute target. If the sea conditions had suddenly deteriorated, however, this could be problematic. On the night of 11–12 February 1942, for example, MGB *314* arrived off Moulin-de-la-Rive in north-western Brittany to extract three operatives – Pierre de Vomécourt ('Lucas'), Mathilde Carré ('The She Cat'), and Ben Cowburn ('Benoit'). Unfortunately, for this mission the vessel possessed just two dinghies instead of surf boats. The dinghies successfully reached the shore and

# Surf Boat

**Maritime vessels extracting operatives from enemy territory (typically, at night) would employ a small boat, such as this surf boat, to take the precious 'cargo' from the shore to the vessel. Surf boats were easy to row and handled well, even in rough seas, unlike dinghies.**

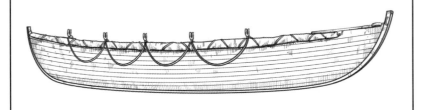

disembarked the two operatives being inserted. However, with the sea conditions quickly deteriorating, when Carré tried to embark, the dinghy capsized; the mission had to be abandoned without a successful extraction, and the Germans soon arrested the two insertees. It took a second trip two weeks later to a different beach nearby to extract the agents. By then Carré was actually a treble agent weaving a complex web of deceit (see *Operative Profile: 'The She Cat'*, below).

Having successfully embarked the operatives, the vessel involved then had to surmount numerous challenges to get home safely; the case study in *Tactics Tip: The Challenges of Extraction by Sea*

# Operative Profile: 'The She Cat'

A nurse during France's 1940 defeat by the German forces, Mathilde Carré subsequently joined the Paris-based Franco-Polish Interallié spy network under the codename 'Victoire'. Arrested by the Germans in November 1941, she was interrogated by the German counter-intelligence NCO Hugo Bleicher. She agreed to work as a double agent for the Germans and betrayed many of her Resistance associates. Released so that she could work again among the Resistance, this time as the mistress of Pierre de Vomécourt ('Lucas'), her duplicity was eventually detected. The two lovers apparently then decided to deceive the Germans. Carré allegedly got Bleicher's permission to be extracted from France with 'Lucas' in February 1942, ostensibly working for Bleicher, but in reality operating as a treble agent for the British by feeding the Germans false information. Once her usefulness to British Intelligence was over, she was imprisoned for the rest of the war before standing trial in France for treason. Sentenced to death in January 1949, but with this commuted to 20 years' imprisonment, she actually served just five years in jail. At her trial, the prosecution famously quoted her diary entry, which stated that her three main passions in life were good food, men and Mozart's *Requiem*.

# MTB (Motor Torpedo Boat)

**Fast, small, and manoeuvrable, maritime small craft such as this Motor Torpedo Boat (MTB) were ideal for night-time extraction of secret operatives from enemy territory.**

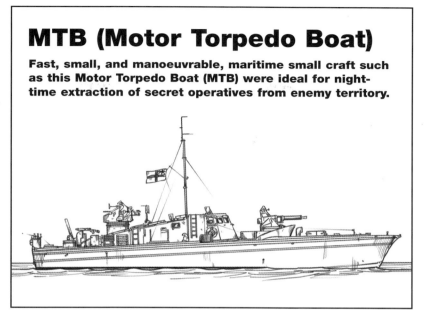

(p288) aptly illustrates these difficulties. The craft might unfortunately encounter an enemy vessel. On 15 April 1944, for example, as MGB *502* extracted 11 personnel from France, she encountered an unidentified enemy vessel that fired on her, killing one crewman. Enemy coastal observers might also spot the vessel, as they did during MGB *502*'s mission of 16 March 1944, leading it to be engaged by coastal artillery. The extraction vessel might also fall foul of the many submerged rocks that littered many parts of the French coast; when 'Brumaire' attempted to escape from Brittany, for example, his small boat was shipwrecked on the Pointe de Raz promontory, after which he was arrested.

## By Land

The third principal method by which Allied special operatives could be extracted from enemy-controlled territory was by land; in other words, operatives (as well as escaped Allied prisoners and downed aircrew) would be taken by guides across the border from France into neutral Spain, from Norway into neutral Sweden, and

# Tactics Profile:
# The Challenges of Extraction by Sea

On the night of 15–16 April 1944, the British D-Class Fairmile Motor Torpedo Boat MTB 718, with MGB 502, journeyed to Brittany to land six SOE operatives with nine suitcases of equipment at the beach of Beg an Fry in Brittany, and then extract 10 operatives. The two gunboats arrived safely off the rendezvous beach and at 01:55 each cast off two surf boats, which took around 20 minutes to reach the shore. The six agents were disembarked safely and the 10 operatives waiting were embarked safely, although the latter's fond farewells delayed the turnaround time from the target five minutes to 10 minutes. After the surf boats reached the gunboats, it took a further 14 minutes to lash them to the gunboats and transfer the operatives on board; both

gunboats then weighed anchor at 13:06. Some minutes later, MGB 502 spotted three enemy patrol vessels at a range of 800m (875 yards). Using the S-Phone, one of the 'Reception Committee' ashore communicated their knowledge of the known local German recognition signals. When challenged by the enemy vessels, the gunboats replied with the recommended signal. Obviously this response was not entirely satisfactory, for the German vessels briefly opened fire, killing one rating. When the Germans failed to keep firing, however, the British crew concluded that the enemy had ultimately accepted the signal as correct. Having avoided the dangerous submerged rocks in the area, the gunboats then had an uneventful return to Dartmouth at 08:08.

MTB 718

# Approaching Border Posts

**Getting an escaping operative through a manned border crossing was an immensely challenging part of the extraction process; it was almost entirely dependent on superior-quality forged papers, a water-tight cover story, the assistance of local guides and/or the bribery of the guards.**

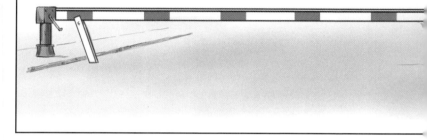

from France, Italy, and Germany into neutral Switzerland. This method of extraction was also laden with difficulties. First, the operatives would have to be guided, or guide themselves, across harsh, remote terrain for considerable distances to approach the border region; this involved all the skills of navigation and self-sufficiency discussed in Chapter 2.

In addition to being a gruelling experience, the operatives ran a constant risk of being discovered by an enemy patrol or betrayed by a local civilian. Even if operatives made it across the border

successfully, neutral countries mounted regular patrols to intercept escaping operatives and prisoners-of-war and intern them. Agent George Bégué, for example, having made it safely into neutral Spain, was arrested and held in the Miranda de Ebro prison camp for two months before being released.

One case study should suffice to highlight the skills and challenges involved in a successful land-based extraction. During March 1942, after his arranged MGB pick-up from Brittany had failed, SOE agent Benjamin Cowburn ('Benoit') linked up with a land-based extraction

border. Here, Cowburn walked many miles across muddy rural terrain to enter Portugal covertly; the next day he was flown back to Britain from Sintra airport.

## Escape from Captivity

Those operatives who escaped from the scene of the mission and were then successfully extracted back to Britain were the lucky ones; many agents were detected by the enemy and captured. All operatives knew what horrors awaited them in enemy hands.

A typical operative's captivity cycle consisted of three distinct phases. Firstly, immediately on being captured, the enemy would march the operative under armed guard to a local holding facility or to some motor transport to take the captive to such a facility. Next, the enemy transported the operative to a regional or national interrogation facility, such as the much-feared Security Police Headquarters on the Avenue Foch in Paris. In the final phase, the enemy would move the operative to one of the infamous German concentration camps like Dachau or Buchenwald.

All phases of this captivity cycle offered some prospects, however remote, of escape. But generally speaking, the level of suffering inflicted upon the operative increased as the individual moved through this cycle, whereas his/her physical capability conversely declined, as did

network in Lyon. After taking a train from Lyon to Toulouse, a Spanish guide took him to Perpignan. That night the two covertly walked south along the railway line, then trekked through the hills before getting some rest in a pigsty; here, they were to link up with another guide and two escapees, but the guide had been fired upon by Spanish border police and lost his clients. Climbing the mountains during the rest of the day, they safely crossed over into Spanish territory. Eventually they made it to the British Consulate in Barcelona, which arranged a car to whisk them to the vicinity of the Portuguese

the possibilities for escape. Therefore, the likelihood of escape was greatest in the earliest phases of captivity. All operatives had undergone specific training in escape tactics, and on occasions agents when captured were able to apply this training despite the unfavourable circumstances in which they found themselves.

## Early Escape

If the operative could master the 'shock of capture' and keep his/her wits, those first few minutes of captivity often offered the most favourable opportunities of escape. If the operative was fortunate, an external source might provide an inadvertent distraction to the guards, for example a casual enquiry from a comrade enquiring who the suspect was. A well-trained operative would likely recognize this fleeting opportunity – it might be now or never.

Indeed, if the operative had not yet been searched thoroughly, he/she may still retain a small penknife or sticker, most probably well-concealed in a sleeve, belt or boot. If all the operatives' weapons had been removed, however, he/she would have to rely on the unarmed combat and silent killing training discussed in the previous chapter. If handcuffed, for example, the operative might manage a boot side kick, smashing his/her boot into the guard's knee and down the shin to bring all his weight down to break the latter's

foot; the agent could then bring his cuffed-hands up for a double-handed chin blow, instantly transformed into an eye gouge. With the guard reeling in agony, the agent ought to have a clear 30 seconds to make good his initial escape. Of course, in real situations operatives combined their training with on-the-spot improvisation.

Operative Robert Maloubier put his early escape training to good effect. On the night of 20 December 1943, for example, German military police arrested Maloubier going out on his motorcycle to recover equipment recently dropped from an Allied aircraft by parachute. With a policeman sitting behind him pressing a gun to his neck, Maloubier had to drive his motorcycle slowly to a nearby police station. Realizing that his chances of escape would only worsen, Maloubier seized his moment just as they neared the station. He simultaneously braked and swerved his bike, throwing off his passenger. Then he picked up and threw the bike at the German as the latter attempted to get up (not something suggested in his training), and dashed off into nearby woods. Despite being in great pain after a round from the German's rifle hit him, Maloubier continued limping on, even dragging himself through waterlogged ditches to put the dogs he could hear pursuing him off his scent. After staggering several miles back to his home, he underwent clandestine surgery and was subsequently evacuated by land across the Spanish border.

Another early opportunity for escape might arise not when the guards had been distracted, but when their route took them over terrain conducive to escape. Such an opportunity might arise, for example, if the guards marched an operative along a bridge that crossed a railway line or road. Timing now was the key to success, as with lightning speed the operative unleashed his unarmed combat skills. If being marched with hands up and the guard pointing a

# Boot Side Kick

**The operative takes his bodyweight on his left foot and, with left knee bent, shoots out his right boot to strike the enemy just below the knee; scraping the enemy's shin downwards, the agent brings his full weight crashing onto the enemy's foot, breaking the small bones; for added impact, the agent could simultaneously inflict a chin-jab on the opponent.**

pistol in his right hand from behind, the operative would suddenly initiate a disarming move. Suddenly turning to the right, the operative passed his right arm over the guard's right forearm near the wrist and placed his/her right hand on his chest, locking and pinning the guard's arm. Simultaneously, the agent brought up his left hand and made a fierce open-hand jab with the back of the hand into the guard's throat, which often forced the opponent to drop the pistol. Once the stunned guard was disarmed, the agent could either instantly flee or finish off the enemy. In the latter case, the agent could then spin the guard around and kill him with a neck-break or a spinal dislocation move.

Next, and without a second's hesitation, the captive would dive over the side of the bridge to fall onto the railway wagons passing underneath. At the moment of impact, the operative would employ his/her extensive parachute training, bending the knees and rolling to the side to absorb the impact of the landing. The last thing an escaping operative needed at this juncture was a broken ankle or knee – an injury that would sound the death-knell to this particular escape bid.

Immediately upon landing, the operative would need to be up and moving, seeking out a location on the moving wagon that afforded better protection from what was about to

# Disarming a Guard from Behind

1. **Suddenly turning to your right, pass your right arm over the guard's right forearm near the wrist and place your right hand on his chest, locking and pinning his arm.**
2. **Bring up your left hand and make an open-hand jab with the back of the hand into the guard's throat, which should force him to drop his pistol.**
3. **Vigorously press your right leg into the outside of the guard's leg to disable him.**

occur; for other nearby guards, having recovered from the initial shock of the escape bid, would no doubt now be bringing rifle fire to bear on the wagons

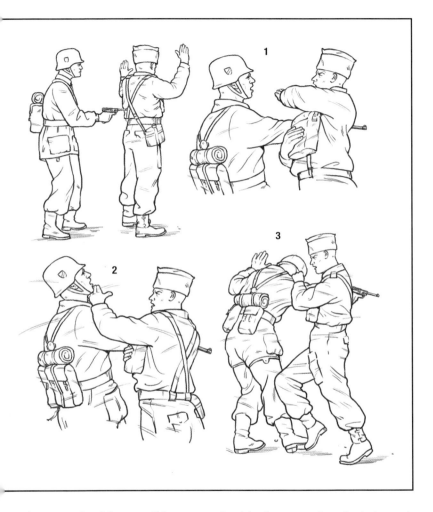

as they moved rapidly away. If the operative could find a place to shelter from this hail of bullets for a short while, then he/she would be safe, at least for the moment, as the train sped beyond effective pistol or rifle range. This first phase of the escape bid had worked; more challenges lay ahead.

# Parachute Roll

**Operatives received parachute landing training, which proved invaluable if, during an escape, an operative had to jump from a height. This training taught the operative to bend at the knees on landing to absorb the initial force of landing and then roll to one side so that the side of the legs, and then the side of the torso, absorbed more gradually the rest of the shock of impact.**

## Escape from Temporary Detention

If no such opportunity arose for the captive operative, or if he/she was still too stunned from injuries incurred at the moment of capture, the operative might find himself in a motor vehicle under armed guard in transit to a temporary detention facility. Again, an external event might fortuitously provide the momentary distraction required for an escape bid. If an oncoming car took the bend too fast, forcing the driver to swerve to take evasive action, this might give the operative a split second to rise up from his/her seat, viciously jab the guard in the chin with an elbow or fist, and throw himself/herself out of the back of the truck. This again was a high-risk strategy; with hands manacled, the operative might sustain fearful injuries as he/she hit the road, even if parachute landing techniques had been employed. Once sprawled on the ground, the operative would need swiftly to be up and running into nearby cover, as enemy fire no doubt now deluged the area.

Once an operative reached a regional or national prison, such as Fresnes Prison or that on Avenue Foch, both in Paris, the chances of successful escape were extremely remote, as such places had tight security and because the captive was, by now, in poor physical shape. Generally, operatives only escaped from such places after seizing a fleeting opportunity during a lapse in the normal high security. When German guards dumped 'Brumaire' unconscious in a fifth-floor attic cell at 84 Avenue Foch with an unbarred window, they no doubt intended to return before he regained his senses. But the battered agent recovered quicker than expected; seizing this fleeting opportunity to escape, he dragged himself across the room and jumped out the window, sadly falling to his death.

In 1943, Agent 'Jacques', despite being blinded during interrogation, managed to seize an opportunity when his tormentors left the room briefly; staggering to his feet, the handcuffed agent leaped through a second-floor window and amazingly managed to escape with the assistance of a sympathetic passer-by. Similarly, at Fresnes Prison, tortured operative Harry Peulevé managed to sidle unnoticed into a crowd of visitors and shuffled out in their midst through the main gate, only to be spotted and shot in the leg.

Another potential vulnerability in such prisons' strict security were the iron bars across the windows of cells. At Avenue Foch, during one cold night, SOE Agents John R. Starr and Noor Khan ('Madeleine') managed to loosen and remove the bars in their attic cell by picking at the surrounding masonry using a screwdriver that

# Escaping Through Concertina Wire

**For an operative escaping from a prison, getting through the surrounding concertina wire was an immense challenge. By using a long pole to lift up the wire's longitudinal coil, a careful and methodical escapee could get through such an obstacle without serious injury, given sufficient time.**

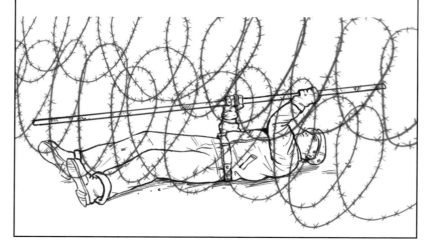

Starr had acquired. Once outside, they escaped across the rooftops. Unfortunately a nearby Allied air raid prompted the Germans to hold an unscheduled roll-call, during which they discovered the missing inmates; in the ensuing searches they were soon recaptured. Many injured escapees received no medical attention – Starr had to go through the agonies of removing the bullet he'd received in his leg when escaping with a spoon!

Yet one operative successfully utilized the desperate strategy of making himself so ill the enemy took him to a civilian hospital, which was less secure. In late 1941 SOE Agent

Major Gerard Morel was arrested by the Vichy French police and held at Périgueux prison; here, he went on hunger strike and having become dangerously ill was transferred to Limoges hospital, where he was operated on. With the stitches still in his stomach, he escaped from the prison hospital and once more crossed the Pyrenees and got back safely to England.

## Escape from Concentration Camps

Once at Nazi concentration camps like Dachau, one would expect that the chances of operative escape were nil. But these camps formed the nexus of a network of smaller satellite labour facilities, on which the collapsing German war economy relied. With hundreds of labour parties leaving from the camp or its satellites

# Crossing Wire

**It is often better to cross under wire than over it. First, dig a channel beneath the wire, wide enough to accommodate your body, then wriggle through the channel, holding the wire up with a piece of non-conducting material.**

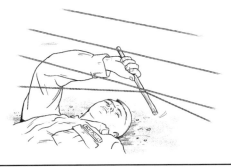

# Prison Camp

Escaping from prison posed numerous challenges for the operative: how to get out of the cells; how to evade the guards while moving towards the perimeter fence; how to get through the fence and wire unobserved; and how to get away quickly and unseen before the escape was discovered.

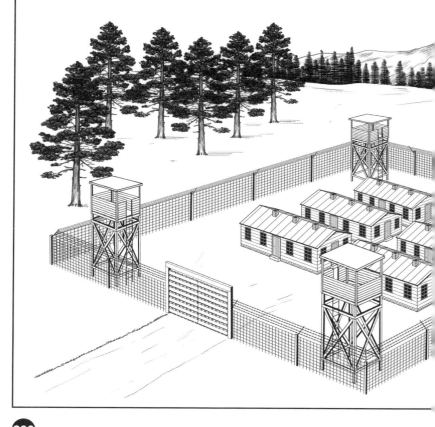

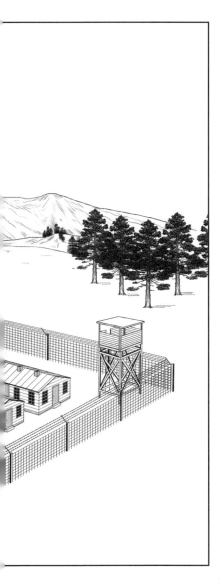

and then returning at the end of the day, and with guard levels reduced by the insatiable demands for replacements at the front, occasionally fleeting opportunities for escape occurred. Moreover, with the Germans moving many thousands of inmates from camp to camp to prevent them being liberated in the war's final weeks, and with the bureaucratic system collapsing, more opportunities for escape emerged. At Buchenwald, two SOE operatives of a group of 37 slated for execution, Forest Yeo-Thomas ('White Rabbit') and Harry Peulevé, managed with the cooperation of some insiders to get new identities and documentation, 'stolen' from prisoners who had died of typhus; the two got sent out to satellite labour camps in their new identities. Peulevé was moved from camp to camp until in the war's final days he escaped from his work party near Magdeburg and eventually met up with advancing American forces. Meanwhile, the Germans had moved 'White Rabbit' by train away from the advancing American forces. When the train stopped for the guards to supervise the inmates burying those captives who had died during the journey, 'White Rabbit' rushed headlong into nearby woods and reached the American lines; only one other agent of this group of 37 sent to Buchenwald survived captivity.

A final way in which an operative might escape enemy captivity was through the actions of friendly forces – in other words, through a rescue mission. Such missions, of course, could only occur if knowledge of the location of a captive could be communicated back to Britain. Incredibly, when wireless operator Major Georges Bégué was held by the Vichy French at Mauzac prison in 1943, he managed to assemble, from oddments passed to him by a sympathetic French guard, a crude radio transmitter. With this he successfully managed to get a faint Morse code message to London informing SOE that he was alive but incarcerated. The wife of one of the Resistance operatives held at Mauzac, Madame Bloch, together with local *Maquisards* and sympathetic camp guards planned and executed an audacious mass-escape plan (*Tactics Tip: An 'Inside' and 'Outside' Job of Prison Escape*, p304).

The Allied armed forces, of course, could also directly assist a planned

# Tactics Tip:
# Aerial Assistance to Operative Prison Escape

Once an operative was in enemy captivity, there was generally only so much that SOE could do to facilitate his/her escape. On several occasions, however, the parent organizations went to considerable lengths to help groups of operatives escape the hands of the Gestapo. On 18 February 1944, for example, 18 RAF de Havilland DH-98 Mosquito fighter-bombers attacked Amiens prison to facilitate the escape of Resistance operatives, 120 of whom were to be executed the next day. The attack breached the walls, permitting 254 to escape (although many were soon recaptured); the attack killed 50 German personnel and, sadly, 40 prisoners. Similarly, on 21 March 1945, 18 RAF Mosquitoes attacked the Gestapo headquarters in Copenhagen, again to facilitate the escape of dozens of Resistance operatives imprisoned there and destroy Gestapo records. The raid allowed 18 prisoners to escape, killed 50 German personnel, 47 Danish Gestapo employees, and sadly seven prisoners and no fewer than 125 innocent civilians in an adjacent building.

prison escape; on several key occasions RAF fighter-bombers attacked enemy prisons to break down the walls and perimeter wire, to allow the operatives held within to escape; two of the most famous such instances are recounted in *Tactics Tip: Aerial Assistance to Operative Prison Escape* (below).

Once the mission had been executed, the operatives involved – as we have seen – had to employ all their skills and resources to escape

the scene and then be safely extracted from behind enemy lines, back to friendly territory. These operatives had to employ their full range of skills and training. They frequently had to combine ingenuity with bravado, courage with determination; they routinely had to employ their navigational and parachute landing drills, their silent killing and unarmed combat training, and their concealment and living-off-the-land capabilities.

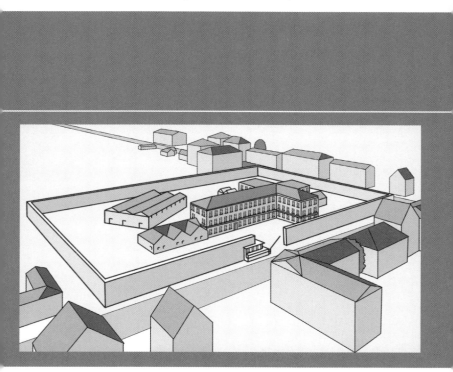

# Tactics Tip:
# An 'Inside' and 'Outside'
# Job of Prison Escape

When wireless operator Major Georges Bégué was held by the Vichy French at Mauzac prison, he participated in a daring and sophisticated mass escape bid that was made possible by the efforts of Resistance activists outside the prison. First, Bégué fashioned a key to open the locks on their cell door using scraps of sardine-can lids, with his co-conspirators holding singing contests to drown the noise of the tools that had been smuggled in to the camp. Then, at the appointed hour on 14 July 1942, Bégué used the duplicate key to unlock the escapees' cells; outside, several guards who had been bribed by the outsiders involved in the plot made themselves scarce. In just 11 minutes, the inmates had made their way out of the prison and under the perimeter wire using wooden trestles they had constructed. Some 15 individuals then crammed into a small car and were taken to a forest, through which they walked to a remote pre-equipped safe house; from there, they subsequently escaped to neutral Spain.

Despite employing all of these skills, however, dozens of operatives, sadly, were captured by the enemy. After heinous torture, incarceration for those operatives who did not manage to pull off the incredible feats of escape described above invariably reached the terrible end of the line – in hell-holes of human degradation like Buchenwald. Yet, even here, some operatives, using all of their guile, and determination, managed to escape or at least contrive to survive until the end of the war. Dozens of emaciated and battered operatives, however, paid the ultimate price for their courage and service behind enemy lines, succumbing to the executioner's bullet or the hangman's noose. Let subsequent generations not forget the bravery and devotion to duty displayed by the special operatives discussed in these chapters.

# Guarded Borders

**The key to getting escaping operatives across a guarded border into a neutral country was to use experienced local guides. With their extensive local knowledge and field-craft skills, these guides would take an operative through remote and difficult terrain to cross the border unobserved, and to safety.**

# FURTHER READING

Anon. *How to be a Spy: The World War II SOE Training Manual* (Toronto: Dundurn, 2001).

Anon. *The Secret Agent's Pocket Manual, 1939–1945* (London: Conway, 2009).

Baden-Powell, D. *Operation Jupiter* (London: Robert Hale, 1982).

Bailey, R. *Forgotten Voices of the Secret War* (London: Ebury, 2008).

Bailey, R. *Baker Street Irregular* (London: Methuen, 1965).

Beevor, J.G. *SOE Recollections and Reflections 1940–45* (London: Bodley Head, 1981).

Bott, Lloyd. *The Secret War from the River Dart* (Dartmouth: Dartmouth History Research Group, 1997).

Boyce, Fredric, and Douglas Everett. *SOE: The Scientific Secrets* (Stroud: Sutton, 2003).

Buckmaster, M. *Specially Employed* (London: Batchworth, 1952).

Casey, William. *The Secret War against Hitler* (London: Simon and Schuster, 1988).

Cookridge, E.H. *Inside SOE* (London: Arthur Barker, 1966).

Crowdry, Terry. *SOE Agent* (Oxford: Osprey, 2008).

Cruickshank, C. *SOE in Scandinavia* (Oxford: OUP, 1986).

Dahl, Per. *Heavy Water and the Wartime Race of Nuclear Energy* (Bristol: Institute of Physics Publishing, 1999).

Davidson, B. *Special Operations Europe* (London: Victor Gollancz 1980).

Dear, Ian. *Sabotage & Subversion* (London: Arms & Armour, 1996).

Dixon, C. Aubrey and Heilbrunn, Otto. *Communist Guerrilla Warfare* (London: Allen and Unwin, 1954).

Dodds Parker, D. *Setting Europe Ablaze* (Windlesham: Springwood Books, 1983).

Escott, Beryl. *The Heroines of SOE F Section* (Stroud: History Press, 2010).

Foot, M.R.D. *SOE in France* (London: HMSO, 1966).

Foot, M.R.D. *Resistance* (London: Paladin, 1976).

Foot, M.R.D. *SOE: The Special Operations Executive 1940–46* (London: BBC, 1984).

Foot, M.R.D. *SOE in the Low Countries* (London: St. Ermin's Press, 2001).

Foot, M.R.D. and J.M. Langley. *MI9: Escape and Evasion 1939–45* (London: The Bodley Head, 1979).

Gardham, Duncan. 'MI5 Files: Nazis plotted to kill Allied troops with coffee', *The Telegraph* (4 April 2011).

Gjelsvik, Tore. *Norwegian Resistance, 1940–1945* (London: Hurst, 1979).

Grau, Lester and Gress, Michael (eds). *The Partisan's Companion, 1942: The Red Army's Do-It-Yourself, Nazi-Bashing Guerrilla Warfare Manual* (Newbury: Casemate, 2011).

Haukelid, Knut. *Skis Against the Atom* (London: William Kimber, 1954).

Howarth, David. *The Shetland Bus* (London: Fontana, 1951).

Irwin, W. *The Jedburghs* (New York: Public Affairs, 2005).

Iversen, Kaare. *Shetland Bus Man* (Lerwick: Shetland times, 2004).

Jespersen, Knud. *No Small Achievement: Special Operations Executive and the Danish Resistance, 1940–1945* (Odense: University Press of Southern Denmark, 2002).

Kurzman, Dan. *Blood and Water: Sabotaging Hitler's Bomb* (New York: Henry Holt, 1997).

Ladd, James and Melton, Keith. *Clandestine Warfare: Weapons and Equipment of SOE and OSS* (London: Blandford, 1988).

Lorraine, Pierre. *Secret Warfare: The Arms and Techniques of Resistance* (London: Orbis, 1983).

Mackenzie, W. *The Secret History of S.O.E.* (London: St Ermin's Press, 2000).

Manus, Max. *Underwater Saboteur* (London: Fontana, 1953).

Marks, Leo. *Between Silk and Cyanide* (London: Harper Collins, 1998).

Michel, Henri. *The Shadow War: Resistance in Europe, 1939–45* (London: Andre Deutsch, 1972).

Miller, Russell. *Behind Enemy Lines* (London: Secker and Warburg, 2002).

Moore, Bob (ed). *Resistance in Western Europe* (Oxford: Berg, 2000).

Moss, W.S. *Ill-Met by Moonlight* (London: Harrap, 1950).

'Obituary, Major Dennis Ciclitira'. *The Telegraph* (16 June 2000).

Richards, Brooks. *Secret Flotillas: Clandestine Sea Operations to Norway, 1940–44* (London: Frank Cass, 2004).

Riste, O. *Norway 1940-45: The Resistance Movement* (Norway: Aschehoug, 1979).

Ruby, Marcel. *F Section SOE* (London: Leo Cooper, 1988).

Saelen, Frithjof. *None but the Brave* (London: Souvenir, 1955).

Seaman, M. *Special Operations Executive* (London: Routledge, 2006).

Slepyan, Kenneth. *Stalin's Guerrillas: Soviet Partisans in World War II* (Lawrence, KS: University Press of Kansas, 2006).

Sønsteby, Gunnar. *Report from No. 24,* (London: Four Square, 1965).

Stafford, David, *Mission Accomplished: SOE and Italy, 1943–45* (London: Bodley Head, 2011).
_____. *Secret Agent* (London: BBC, 2000).

Turner, Des. *SOE's Secret Weapons Centre: Station 12* (Stroud: History Press, 2006).

Valentine, Ian. *Station 43: Audley End House and SOE's Polish Section* (Stroud: History Press, 2010).

Verity, Hugh. *We Landed by Moonlight* (Manchester: Crecy, 2000).

Von Dach Bern, H. *Total Resistance* (Bolder, Colorado: Paladin, 1965).

Weale, Adrian. *Secret Warfare* (London: Coronet, 1997).

West, Nigel. *Secret War, The Story of SOE* (London: Hodder & Stoughton, 1992).

White, Terry. *Fighting Techniques of the Special Forces* (London: Century, 1993).

# INDEX

Page numbers in *italics* refer to illustrations